Warman's
Weller Pottery

DENISE RAGO AND DAVID RAGO

Identification and Price Guide

©2007 Krause Publications

Published by

krause publications

An Imprint of F+W Publications

700 East State Street • Iola, WI 54990-0001
715-445-2214 • 888-457-2873
www.krausebooks.com

Our toll-free number to place an order or obtain a free catalog is (800) 258-0929.

Library of Congress Catalog Number: 2006935765
ISBN: 978-0-89689-468-6

Designed by Donna Mummery
Edited by Kristine Manty

Printed in China

Acknowledgments

Thanks to my father and Suzanne for giving me an education few are lucky enough to have, Todd and Emma for the countless ways in which you helped with this book, to Barbara Gerr and Arnie Small for your generosity in sharing photos of your collection for this publication, Anthony Barnes, Lynnette Mager, and Eliane Talec for your assistance in putting this together, and to my family and friends for your love and support.

Contents

Introduction

It looks like Samuel Weller's time has finally come. His famous pottery by the same name slugged it out with several other important Zanesville, Ohio potteries for decades. Cross-town rivals such as Roseville, Owens, La Moro, and McCoy were all serious fish in a fairly small and well-stocked lake. While Mr. Weller occasionally landed some solid body punches with many of his better art lines, the prevailing thought was that his later production ware just wasn't up to snuff.

There was a lot of evidence to support such beliefs. Roseville, after all, came out with three distinctly different eras of production-oriented pottery, consisting of lines which had decoration either applied with transfers (decals), including many of its cream ware lines, or lines where the decorative elements were embossed in the mold and then quickly colored by hand to give the appearance of individuality, including Falline, Columbine, and Magnolia. Roseville excelled at producing such relatively inexpensive ware.

Though it was almost certainly not Roseville's original intent, the company's creation of easily distinguished and codified offerings such as Sunflower and Pinecone were to become perfect collecting fodder 50 years after they were originally produced. There were more than 100 variations on the Pinecone theme, each available in three distinctly different colors. When Martha Stewart started collecting Sunflower, well, this is no small thing.

Modern ceramic collectors usually don't begin with a purchase of a high end, multi-thousand dollar art piece. Instead, collecting art pottery usually begins with an attraction toward, and a purchase of, a more modestly priced molded pot. The Owens pottery, which folded shortly after J.B.'s death in 1907, never got around to developing such easily affordable lines. While Owens early art ware was as creative and interesting as anything made in Zanesville, I'm convinced that its marketability is persistently difficult today because of so little of the existing work is available at entry-level prices.

Samuel Weller was a notorious copier and, it is said, a bit of a scallywag. He paid designers such as William Long to bring their famous discoveries to Zanesville. He then attempted to steal their secrets, and, when successful, renaming them and making them his own. You might imagine that he lacked original thought. And you might assume from all this that he was reactive and not creative. You might be wrong.

It's difficult to say whether the chicken or the egg came first at the potteries of the Ohio valley. After World War I, when the cost of materials became less expensive than the cost of labor, many companies, including the famous Rookwood Pottery, increased their output of this less expensive production ware. What is clear is that Weller Pottery followed along in the trend of production ware by introducing scores of interesting and unique lines, the likes of which have never been created anywhere else, before or since.

Yet, in addition to a number of noteworthy production lines, Weller continued in the creation of

Many lines of Weller were hand painted and often signed by important artists. This Hudson vase features a finely painted scenic by Hester Pillsbury, with a mountainous landscape, stamped mark and artist's signature, 12" h, **$4,500-$5,500**.

hand-painted ware long after Roseville abandoned them. Some of the more interesting Hudson pieces, for example, are post World War I pieces. Even later lines, such as Bonito, were hand painted and often signed by important artists such as Hester Pillsbury. The closer you look at Weller's output after 1920, the more obvious the fact that it was the only Zanesville company still producing both quality art ware and quality production ware.

Current pricing of and interest in Weller pottery has shown a tremendous growth of interest in its work, well above that of the other Zanesville potteries. The purpose of this book is to show this renewed interest in Weller pottery both in terms of its historic backdrop and current market appeal. This reassessment is long overdue. Nevertheless, this book is itself a response to the market trends that have become apparent in the last two years. While there has long been a market for such favorite Weller production lines as Glendale, Woodcraft, and Coppertone, the interest has been spread across the board, excepting some of its last work, mostly an assortment of World War II-era flower shop pottery.

Another purpose of this introduction is to introduce to you my daughter, Denise Rago-Wallace, who you should safely assume was predestined to have an interest in American decorative ceramics. One of her earliest road trips as a child included a visit to the Zanesville Pottery Lovers Festival, the Mecca for all things Weller. She grew up around art pottery and, at

an early age, was comfortable being around it.

She began her professional career managing our on-line, 24/7 ceramic auction and information site which, in spite of her efforts, educated us about how little we knew about dedicated Internet auctions. Several years back, Denise became manager of our semi-annual Zanesville auctions, with sole responsibility for vetting and staging the event. These have been, and remain, the benchmark for selling Zanesville pottery at auction. In addition to the production of all-color catalogues, her auctions pioneered the use of NXT technology, with the first fully operational electronic sales brochure.

Several records were established at these sales, including $20,000 for an early production line Tourist wall pocket and $39,000 for a large Della Robbia vase with daffodils. These prices, and those of thousands of pieces, are available for view online, for free, on our searchable database at Ragoarts.com.

I encourage you to read, ask, and scour the available information at our site and the others listed at the back of this book. And I hope that the pursuit of this often lovely and rare decorative ware rewards you not only with the excitement found in discovering a good piece, but in the relationships you develop with other collectors and dealers along the way.

David Rago

Coppertone pieces are among those that are a favorite with collectors. This Coppertone bowl has a frog perched on lily pads, has a stamped mark and is 4-1/4" x 11", **$300-$500.**

Guide To Buying

While no one can accurately predict the future of the Weller market, several factors can contribute to the value and desirability of a piece.

Size

Large forms, 12 inches or taller, are more likely to retain or increase in value than the smaller examples. Large examples are far less common for several reasons: They were produced primarily for exhibitions, or to be given as presentation items, consuming a lot of the artist's time and attention. They were expensive even at that time, and were considered to be luxury items. Small pieces were manufactured in greater quantity because they utilized less artistry, making them less costly to produce.

Small pieces were not as prone to breakage during the production process, and were more likely to have survived without damage through the years. For example, a cabinet vase usually stayed in the cabinet, whereas a floor vase was out in the open and susceptible to damage.

Form

The form itself is also important. A vase will almost always bring more than a bowl, ewer, or teapot. In production lines, baskets are quite popular, along with lidded jars and wall pockets. Pieces that aren't relevant today have become increasingly less desirable, such as oil lamps and cuspidors.

Decoration

Finely decorated, artist-signed pieces stand out from the others. Those with common decoration, such as grapes or wild roses, pale in comparison to those with bats, cats, or cabins. A Hudson vase signed by Hester Pillsbury is far more saleable than a vase lacking the artist's signature. Only rarely will a truly exceptional example of art ware be found without the artist's cipher, or even better a full signature, so the mark is usually a good indication of decorative quality.

Pillow vase, Sicard, scalloped rim, perfectly fired, marked Weller Sicard on body, 9", **$1,500-$2,500.**

Chilcote signature.

Vase, Hudson, finely painted by Mae Timberlake with poppies in blue, pink, and ivory, stamped mark and artist's signature, 12" x 6-1/2", **$1,500-$2,500**. This style of floral decoration is particularly popular with buyers.

Vase, Hudson, bulbous, two-handled, painted by Sarah Reid McLaughlin with white and yellow roses, stamped mark and artist's mark, 7-3/4", **$600-$800**.

Weller's colorful and complex glazes easily mask hairlines, making close inspection a necessity.

It is understandably difficult for those new to the Weller market to separate the run-of-the-mill decoration from the outstanding, but with a little research and experience, it becomes easy to divide the two. Several other resources are noted at the end of this book if you are interested in learning more.

With all the information available to buyers today, it is easy to arm yourself with knowledge before putting your money on the table. Unfortunately, all this knowledge isn't enough to guarantee you will make a sound purchase. Nothing can replace experience when it comes to spotting damage and repairs, and even with many years of experience, it's not uncommon for a good restoration or a tight crack to go unnoticed.

Condition

The condition of a piece is a major factor. A ceramic in perfect shape will attract a broader clientele than those with any type of post-factory damage. Please see our guide to assessing damage for an in-depth look at condition and how it affects value, Page 13.

You will discover that several lines are nearly impossible to find in mint condition, such as Jap Birdimal and Turada. With the squeezebag decoration to both lines, and the many high points on the reticulated design of Turada, it is rare to find an example without minor damage. Collectors are more forgiving with this type of piece, and slight flaws such as flecks to the tube-lining or squeezebag decoration, or glaze scaling to the edges, are more often overlooked. On the other hand, when a truly perfect example comes up for auction, collectors are willing to pay a premium.

Turada pieces without minor damage are rare to find. This Turada bowl is tapered with a wide floral band, and reticulated medallions all in orange and blue squeezebag on a dark green ground, 3", **$150-$250.**

Marks

Another important factor collectors should familiarize themselves with is the markings found on Weller pottery. There are many different markings found on pieces and here are some examples.

Incised script mark.

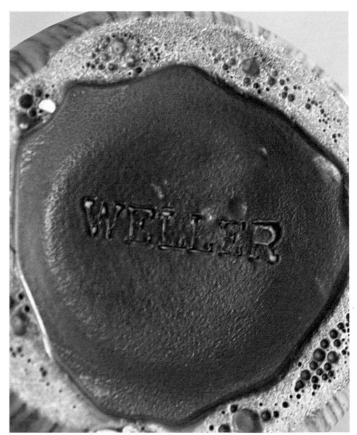

Impressed WELLER mark.

Ink stamp mark.

Rhead Faience incised mark.

Incised script mark on a Patra vase.

Incised script mark on a star vase.

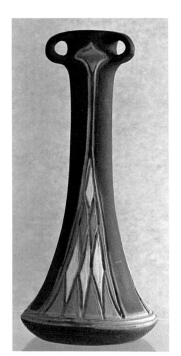

Incised corseted vase.

Another variation of the incised Rhead Faience mark.

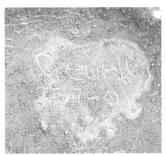

This is an example of the etched marking found on Clewell's metal-covered pieces; this particular piece was produced using a Weller blank.

A very rare raised mark, found on a Stellar vase.

One of several black stamp marks used by Weller.

Impressed numerals found on several of their forms.

Occasionally a piece will be found with a sequence of numbers in crayon or pencil.

Marks can be very hard to see, making some pieces difficult to identify. This rare vase has a very faint impressed WELLER mark.

Vase, Louwelsa, finely painted by Elizabeth Blake with a Saint Bernard, impressed mark and artist's signature, 10-1/2" x 6", **$700-$900**. Prices for Louwelsa pieces have decreased over the past 20 years

It is also wise to get ahead of the trends in the ceramic market. While a piece may not be particularly desirable today, it may be tomorrow. If you purchase a currently underappreciated piece at its lowest price point, you'll often see the value rise as trends fluctuate.

Louwelsa and Aurelian, two of Weller's brown-glazed lines, were popular in the 1970s and 1980s during the rise of the Weller Pottery collector's market, but have substantially decreased in value since that time. Today's prices seem very low in comparison to their price 20 years ago.

Pricing note

While following all the guidelines previously listed should give you a good start, there is no better way to collect Weller than to buy what you love. As with any investment, there is no guaranteed return on your money. If you purchase a piece you would enjoy looking at on the shelf each day, its latent value becomes far less important. An investment in the stock market can't be kept in a showcase, or passed on amongst family members. Pottery is to be enjoyed and admired for its history and artistry. The potential profit to be made should be secondary.

The values in this book are based on auction values alone, as I have worked solely in auctions for nearly 10 years. I've found it is the easiest way to gauge the ups and downs of the market, using online resources such as Artfact to trace the sale of a single item through nearly 20 years of auction records.

Book value can sometimes give readers an inflated idea of value. For example, a piece valued at $1,700 in 1986 is not necessarily going to be worth the same or more in 2007. When comparing current values to prices listed in earlier books, you will sometimes find the lines have decreased in value over time. People assume that a piece of Louwelsa estimated at $2,000-$2,500 in the 1980s is worth at least $3,000 today. In all actuality, you will probably only get $800 for that same piece, due to the current lack of interest in brown-glazed lines.

Please use the values listed as a general guideline, allowing room for the ups and downs of an ever-changing market. Every price guide has a shelf life, and applies only to a limited area of the market. You may get a deal on a piece at a show from someone to looking to liquidate inventory, or you could pay twice its presumed value because it is one of a kind. You may pay half the low estimate at auction, or double the high because you are competing against one other determined bidder. A piece is only worth what one or two people are willing to pay for it. If you are looking to purchase a piece, it is ultimately up to you to determine its value.

Please see the chapters on Early Art Ware and Middle Period to Later Commercial Ware for a more detailed look at the best buys of the Weller market.

How to use this book

This book is divided into two sections: Early Art Ware, and Middle Period to Late Art Ware and Commercial Ware. Pottery lines in each section are listed alphabetically, and a brief summary of characteristics and production dates are given. Photographs are also in alphabetical order by form.

Condition and Assessing Damage

You should look for the following types of post-factory damage or factory flaws when purchasing pottery.

Crazing is a crackled pattern that is almost always caused in the firing process, although it can also happen with age, or with improper care. Generally it is not considered a flaw, and will not detract from a piece's value unless it becomes dark or begins to separate. Separation may occur if you use a bleach product to clean pottery without thoroughly rinsing it, and it can also separate if it is left outside to freeze in cold winter months. This can destroy its entire value, so be sure to use liners in your planters and vases, and reserve them for indoor use if you live in an area with very cold winter weather.

A hairline can vary from a dark crazing line to tight crack. A minor hairline would be short and fine, while a major one might extend through the entire body. The line can sometimes be lightened by soaking it for an extended period of time, using very hot water and liquid dishwashing soap. A minor hairline only causes a slight reduction in value, although where there is one hairline, another often opposes it. One person's idea of a hairline can be very different from the next, so be careful when buying pieces describes as having hairlines, unless you're inspecting it in person.

A crack is considered to be a more serious hairline, sometimes with separation or small slivers of clay missing. It can cause a piece to become unstable, which reduces the value of the piece greatly. A large crack needs to be stabilized in order to prevent further damage. This can be done by a professional restoration artist, who can best be found by word of mouth at pottery shows or discussion groups. The cost of restoration can greatly vary depending on the damage, the time frame in which the repair needs to be done, and the overall quality of the restoration and the restorer.

A chip can be either very minor or serious, depending on its size, cause, or location.

A grinding chip is caused when a piece of pottery is scraped off the kiln, and small pieces of the glaze or clay are pulled off along with it.

A stilt-pull chip is created when the three-prong stilt used to lift pottery off of the kiln floor during firing

 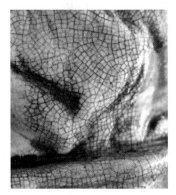

Camelot detail crazing.   Crazing detail.

becomes stuck to the clay or glaze inside the foot ring, pulling a piece off. This type of chip is not considered a serious flaw, unless it causes the piece to become unstable or unsightly.

A re-glued chip detracts slightly less value than a chip, because there is less to fill-in or repair. A handle is much easier re-glued than recreated entirely. If you plan to have a piece of pottery restored, the fragments are best left un-glued. Your restorer will have the proper tools to reattach any broken parts.

Drill holes are fairly common because it was an inexpensive way for someone to make a lamp from a vase. It is not a very serious form of damage, so long as it was not drilled in any area other than the bottom. These can be easily restored and would only lose approximately 20 percent of their original value, but

Vase, Louwelsa, bulbous, fitted as a lamp base, and painted with flowers in brown and yellow, impressed mark, pottery: 10-1/2", **$50-$75**, with a post-factory drill-hole.

Small chips or "nicks" to the edges of a Weller swan figure.

it is important that the restoration does not cover any important dates or artist's marks.

A proper restoration can often also restore a good amount of value caused by damage, depending on the extent of the original damage and the quality of the repair. Certain types of pieces are more easily restored than others, with glossy lines being more difficult to mask a repair. A high-quality repair can only be seen by the trained eye, but it can be very costly. The value of the piece, monetary or sentimental, should always be greater than the cost of the repair. A poor restoration is difficult to un-do, and can devalue a piece further if done improperly or sloppily.

A glaze miss is a small area of clay that was not covered when glaze was applied.

A kiln kiss is a spot on the glaze where a pot was pressed against something during the firing process. These are rare on Weller, but when found, are often on the side of the body over a decorated area, and might keep pickier buyers from adding it to their collection.

Peppering is a black "peppered" or dotted discoloration to a piece, sometimes heavily concentrated in one small area, other times lightly spread across the entire body. Unless it is severe, it is considered to be a common factory variance rather than a flaw.

Burst bubbles are common and acceptable, but large bubbles or those over a decorated area can deter buyers from paying top dollar.

Firing lines are cracks created during the firing process, often forming where applied decorations and handles connect to the body. Firing lines can be differentiated from standard cracks because the glaze often seeps inside and darkens while it's being fired. Most firing lines won't deter even the pickiest of buyers, but some will cause instability or can be unsightly, which will devalue a piece slightly.

Damage doesn't detract an exact amount of value from every piece. It depends on the rarity of the item, the location and extent of damage, and whether or not the piece is easily fixable, along with many other factors. When pressed to put a number on it, post-factory damage of any sort detracts a minimum of 20 percent of the value. Large chips or cracks could devalue it by 90 percent.

Production Dates

The following is a chronological order of when Weller's various pottery lines were produced:

Early Art Ware

1896-1924	Louwelsa
1897-1898	Dickensware 1 (Dickens Ware)
1897-1898	Turada
1898-1910	Aurelian
1898	Auroro
1898 to 1915-1918	Eocean
1900-1905	Dickensware II
1902-1907	Sicard
1903	Jap Birdiman and Rhead Faience
1903-1904	Dickensware III
1903-1904	L'Art Nouveau
1903 or 1904	Fudzi
1904	Floretta
1904	Hunter
1904	Matt Floretta
1904	Perfecto and Matt Louwelsa
1905	Fru Russet / Weller Matt
1905	Etched Matt
1905	Matt Green
Sometime between 1905 and 1910	Dresden
1906	Etna
Sometime before 1910	Greenaways
1910	Etched Floral or Molded Etched Matt

Middle Period to Late Art Ware and Commercial Ware

1910	Burntwood and its "sister-line" Claywood
1910	Cameo Jewell
1910	Souevo
Sometime between 1910-1914	Xenia
1913	Camelot
Before 1914	Clinton Ivory
1914-late 1920s	Roma
1915	Muskota
1915	Teakwood (a variation of the Burtwood and Claywood line)
Around 1915	Athens
1915	Bedford Glossy and Bedford Matt
1915	Blue Drapery
1915	Brighton
1915	Butterflies, birds, bugs and bees
1915	Copra
1915	Creamware and several variations
1915	Fairfield
1915	Frosted Matt
1915	Louella
1915	Minerva
1915	Orris
1915-1920	Baldin
1915-1920	Florala
Mid-teens-1928	Flemish
Mid-teens-1928	Forest
Around 1916 (possibly 1906)	Jewell
Late teens	Dupont
Late teens	Knifewood and the variation Selma
Late teens-late 1920s	Rosemont
Prior to 1920	Blue Ware
Prior to 1920	Bronze Ware
Prior to 1920	Fruitone
Prior to 1920	Kenova
Prior to 1920	Woodrose
1920	Clairmont
1920	Lustre
1920	Tivoli
1920	Zona
1920-1925	Besline
1920-1925	Lamar
1920-1925	LaSa
1920-1925	Marengo
1920-1928	Ardsley
1920 1933	Woodcraft
Early 1920s	Blue and Decorated and White and Decorated
Early 1920s	Hudson Perfecto
Early 1920s-1928	Pumila
Early 1920s-1928	Voile
Early to late 1920s	Hobart
Early to late 1920s	Klyro
Through the 1920s	Glendale
Through the 1920s	Silvertone
1921	Cloudburst
Early 1920s-mid 1930s	Hudson and variations including Gray-on-Gray and Hudson Light

Early 1920s-1935	Rochelle
1924	Parian
Mid-1920s-1933	Marvo
Late 1920s	Ansonia
Late 1920s	Barcelona
Late 1920s	Chase
Late 1920s	Coppertone
Late 1920s	Sabrinian
Late 1920s	Tutone
Late 1920s	Warwick
Late 1920s-1931	Blo' Red
Late 1920s-early 1930s	Juneau
Late 1920s-1933	Malverne/Malvern
Late 1920s-1933	Patra
Late 1920s-1933	Turkis
1925-1936	Chengtu
1927-1933	Bonito
1928-1933	Velva
Mid to late 1920s-1941	Graystone Garden Ware
1930s	Novelty
Early 1930s	Elberta
Early 1930s	Greora
Early 1930s	Patricia
Early to mid-1930s	Wild Rose
Early 1930s-1934	Manhattan
Early 1930s-1935	Classic
1933	Cornish
1933	Neiska
1934-late 1930s	Atlas
1934	Cretone
1934	Geode and Stellar
1935	Mammy
1935	Paragon
Mid-1930s	Pierre
1935-late 1930s	Cameo

Other lines

1903-1904	Monochrome
1903-1904	Golbogreen or Golbrogreen
1910	Luxor
Sometime after 1910	Lebanon
Sometime after 1910	Reno
1914	Marbelized
1915	Scandia
1915	Underglaze Blue Ware
Late teens	Pearl
1920	Arcola

1920	Eclair
1920	Melrose
1920	Noval
Early 1920s-1928	Lavonia
Early to late 1920s	Breton
Before 1924	Mirror Black
Early 1920s-1928	Florenzo
Mid-1920s-1928	Lorbeek
1928	Alvin
Late 1920s	Dynasty
Late 1920s	Montego
Early 1930s	Cactus
Early 1930s	Candis
Early 1930s	Greenbriar
1930s	Nile
Early 1930s-1935	Softone
Early 1930s-1936	Rudlor
Mid to late 1930s	Arcadia
Mid to late 1930s	Loru
Mid to late 1930s	Panella
Mid to late 1930s	Roba
Mid-1930s to late 1930s	Pastel
1933	Brown and White

Chelsea Utility Ware – 1933

1933	Seneca
1933-1938	Ivoris
1934	Raceme
1935	Darsie
1935	Ragenda
1935-1938	Mi-Flo
Mid- to late 1930s	Blossom
Mid to late 1930s	Delsa
1935-late 1930s	Lido
Sometime prior to 1936	Oak Leaf
Sometime after 1936	Gloria

Kitchen Gem – After 1936

Late 1920s	Decorated Creamware
Late 1920s	Fleron
Late 1920s	Velvetone
Late 1920s-1933	Golden Glow
Late 1920s-1933	Sydonia
After 1936	Raydance
1937	Dorland
1937	Floral
1937	Senic
Late 1930s	Bouquet

Early Art Ware

Weller Pottery created a wide variety of ceramics, from high-end art ware to utilitarian and commercial ware. From the company's early years, Samuel Weller strived to provide a high-quality ceramic, while keeping up with the public's high demand for new glazes and forms. He was able to stay on top of the market by collaborating with potters and artists from around the world, each integrating their personal decorating styles and techniques. For example, William Long played a major part in creating the dark brown blended glaze and decorating techniques, ultimately used to create the Louwelsa line. Charles Upjohn, influenced by both his studies and apprenticeship in Europe, created two Dickensware lines. Henry Schmidt designed the company's first squeezebag or slip-trail line, Turada. Squeezebag, also known as tube lining, is a raised decoration applied by squeezing glaze through a small hole in an instrument, much like decorating a cake.

Jacques Sicard and Henri Gellie brought a highly secretive nacreous glaze used in the Sicardo line, and John Lessell, the metallic lustered glazes used on the commercial ware. Frederick Hurten Rhead, Charles Chilcote, and Claude Leffler, among many other highly-regarded artists, left their impression at Weller before moving on to make their mark at other pottery companies, including Roseville, Homer Laughlin, Arequipa, Clifton, Denver China & Pottery and University City, to name a few.

Early art ware lines are listed alphabetically. For a chronological order of when these pottery lines were introduced, see Production Dates on Pages 15-16.

AURELIAN

As production of the Dickens Ware and Turada lines both ended in 1898, the Aurelian line was developed. Produced until 1910, it is very similar to the Louwelsa line, but the splash of gold, orange, and deep blue streaked glaze sets it apart. Over the bright yellow to brown blended background, the hand-painted and often ornate decorations vary from hunting scenes to delicate flowers. Corleone is considered to be a variation of the Aurelian line, the background with streaked green glaze instead of gold. Aurelian has slightly more value than Louwelsa, although its prices have declined alongside Louwelsa over the years.

Ewer, Aurelian, ruffled rim, painted by T.J. Wheatley with nasturtium, 10", **$500-$700**.

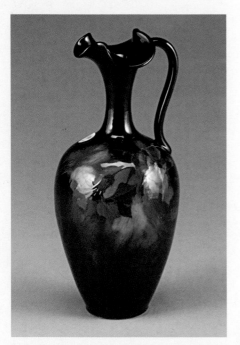

Ewer, Aurelian, painted with orange carnations, impressed Aurelian mark, 11-1/2", **$400-$600**.

Pitcher, Aurelian, squat, painted with small orange flowers and green leaves, impressed mark, 5-1/2" x 5-3/4", **$200-$300**.

Pedestal, Aurelian, twisted, painted by Frank Ferrell with grapes, artist signed, 26" x 10-1/2", **$400-$600**.

Pedestal, Aurelian, twisted, painted with palm fronds, unmarked, 26" x 10-1/2", **$300-$500**.

Pedestal, Aurelian, twisted, painted by Todd Steele with blackberries, 34" x 8", **$450-$650**.

Vase, Aurelian, twisted, faceted painted with carnations, incised mark, 7-1/2" x 6", **$250-$350**.

AURELIAN

Vase, Aurelian, bulbous, painted with clover blossoms, incised mark, 5-1/2" x 3-1/2", **$300-$400**.

Vase, Aurelian, tapered, finely painted with berries and leaves, impressed mark, 9-1/2" x 4", **$250-$350**.

Vase, Aurelian, classically shaped, painted with blossoms and berries, incised mark and illegible artist's initials, 10-1/4" x 4", **$350-$550**.

Vase, Aurelian, ovoid, painted by Frank Ferrell with poppies, incised mark, stamped mark, and artist's initials, 17", **$750-$1,250**.

Vase, Aurelian, tall ovoid, finely painted by R. G. Turner with a full-figure portrait of a monk, incised mark and artist's signature, 19" x 6-3/4", **$1,500-$2,000**.

Also called Auroral, Auroro was introduced sometime around 1898. The production dates of this line are unclear, but the pieces are so scarce, it is likely production was brief. The background color is lightly brushed on in pale pink, blue, green, or yellow. There is a very competitive buyer's market due to its rarity, particularly for pieces with unusual decorations, with goldfish being one of collectors' favorites.

Vase, Auroro, light blue, ovoid, incised mark, 9", **$800-$1,200**.

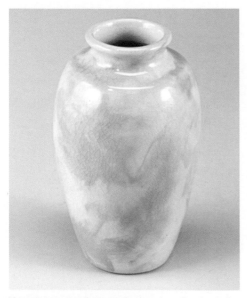

Vase, Auroro, undecorated other than the shaded blue background, incised mark, 6-1/2", **$500-$700**.

Vase, Auroro-type, very finely decorated in unusual colors, 9-1/4", **$3,000-$4,000**.

DICKENSWARE 1 (DICKENS WARE)

It is rumored that Samuel Weller had a hand in naming this line, although it seems more likely that Charles Upjohn, who spent time studying in Charles Dickens' homeland of England, was the sole creator of the name and design ideas. The line is similar in style to Louwelsa, but the background colors used are very dark shades of blue, green, gray, and brown, rather than the blended brown and yellow glazes of Louwelsa. Most often the pieces are slip-painted with flowers, but occasionally they can be found with other painted designs including somewhat crude portraits. The rarity of this line should warrant high selling prices, but the flat, ordinary decoration on these pieces generates little interest. One variation of this early line has a shaded deep chocolate ground painted with gold swirls, and often, clusters of colorful flowers. This particular style of the Dickensware I line is the most collectible, with even the smallest of pieces attracting many competitive buyers.

Vase, Dickensware I, bulbous, beautifully decorated by Frank Ferrell with chrysanthemums in polychrome, impressed mark and signed Ferrell, 7" x 6-1/2", **$1,500-$2,500.**

Jardinière, Dickensware I, painted with nasturtium on a dark green ground, impressed mark and illegible artist's cipher, 11-1/2" x 7-1/2", **$300-$400.**

Jardinière, Dickensware I, painted with orange flowers, impressed mark, 8-1/2" x 11", **$250-$350.**

Large lamp base, Dickensware I, painted by C. J. Dibowski with large cactus blossoms in yellow and amber, complete with original oil lamp font, artist signed and impressed 350, 17-1/2" x 12", **$650-$850**.

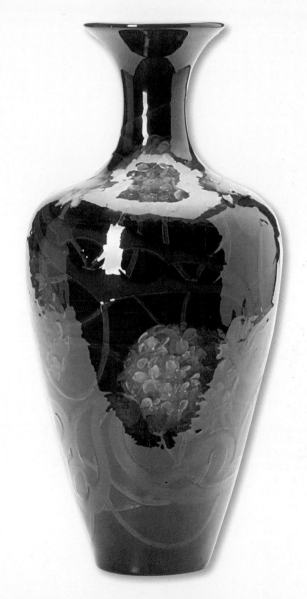

Vase, Dickensware I, four-sided, incised and painted with tulips and yellow scrolled design, impressed 672, 9-1/4" x 6", **$450-$650**.

Vase, Dickensware I, tall baluster, finely painted by Frank Ferrell with clusters of blue and yellow hydrangea, impressed mark, signed Ferrell, 13-1/2" x 6-1/4", **$1,500-$2,500**.

DICKENSWARE II

Designed by Charles Upjohn, Dickensware II was produced from 1900-1905. Each piece was etched with a needle, and the designs were then hand-painted, and finally covered in a glossy or matt glaze.

The figural tobacco jars were also offered with this line, including such figures as "The Captain" and "The Irishman."

A lot of time and care was taken to create each piece, and while the values of the Dickensware II pieces have been steady for several years, the prices do not seem to reflect the workmanship involved in their production.

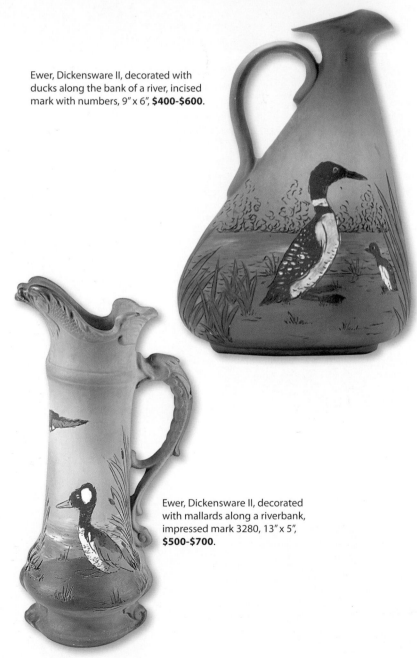

Ewer, Dickensware II, decorated with ducks along the bank of a river, incised mark with numbers, 9" x 6", **$400-$600.**

Ewer, Dickensware II, decorated with mallards along a riverbank, impressed mark 3280, 13" x 5", **$500-$700.**

Ewer, Dickensware II, extremely rare and unusual, shows a golfer and caddy along a deeply incised line of trees. It is one of the finest examples of a golfer I've seen, and would have sold for a considerable amount had this decoration been found on a vase form, with artist's signature (which it lacked). Impressed mark, 11" x 5", **$3,000-$4,000.**

Humidor, Dickensware II, Turk etched mark, 7-1/4" x 6-1/2", **$850-$1,250**.

Jug, Dickensware II by A.H., incised with a monk and painted with chains of flowers, impressed Dickensware Weller mark, artist's initials, 6", **$350-$500**.

Two Dickensware II pieces: a tall ewer covered in sheer glossy blue glaze, incised with a scene and quote from the Pickwick Papers, and a small bulbous jug with incised design, both bear Dickensware impressed mark; ewer: 12-1/4" x 5", **$350-$550**; jug: **$200-$350**.

Mug, Dickensware II, corseted with dolphin handle and molded, stylized band near rim, the body incised with swimming carp in polychrome on a blue and green ground, impressed mark, 6-1/2" x 4-1/4", **$300-$500**.

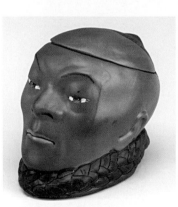

Humidor, Dickensware II Chinaman, incised mark, 6-1/4" x 6", **$1,000-$1,500**.

Pillow vase, Dickensware II, incised and painted with a mallard on a shore, very similar to a Hunter piece in matt glaze, impressed mark and several artist's marks including Charles Upjohn, 5" x 5-1/2", **$400-$600**.

Tall pitcher, Dickensware II, "Captain Duttle Gives Them The Lovely Pea," stamped mark, 12-1/2" x 7", **$450-$650**.

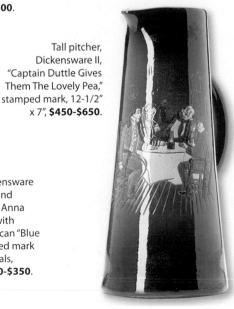

Mug, Dickensware II, incised and painted by Anna Dautherty with Native American "Blue Hawk," impressed mark and artist's initials, 5-1/2" x 5", **$250-$350**.

Vase, Dickensware II, three-sided, incised with swimming fish on a dark green-blue ground, impressed mark, 7" x 4-3/4", **$350-$500**.

DICKENSWARE II

Vase, Dickensware II, has an incised portrait of a Native American, "Black Bird," impressed mark, 7-3/4", **$450-$650**.

Vase, Dickensware II, bulbous, incised and painted with an Indian chief on a robin's egg blue ground, impressed mark, 9", **$1,500-$2,000**.

Vase, Dickensware II, cylindrical, with a golfer missing his club, and trees, etched and artist's marks, 7-1/2" x 2-1/4", **$650-$850**.

Vase, Dickensware II, bulbous, exceptionally decorated by Carl Weigelt with a classical scene, impressed mark and artist's initials, 10", **$1,500-$2,500**.

Vase, Dickensware II, cylindrical, shows male golfer in mid-swing, crisply carved and detailed, impressed mark, 9-1/4" x 3-1/4", **$1,500-$2,500**.

Vase, Dickensware II, corseted, decorated with a lady golfer, signed KP, 10-1/2", **$1,500-$2,500**.

DICKENSWARE II

DICKENSWARE III

Vase, Dickensware II, incised and painted portrait of a Native American, by Edwin Pickens, 10-1/4", **$1,250-$1,500**.

Vase, Dickensware II, decorated with a deer near trees, impressed Dickensware mark, 11-1/4" x 4-1/4", **$1,250-$1,750**.

Vase, Dickensware II, tall, decorated with scene from David Copperfield, 17", **$1,000-$1,500**.

The third Dickensware line was designed by Frederick Hurten Rhead and offered to the public from 1903-1904. It can be easily distinguished from the other two lines. Many of the forms are shared with the Eocean line, along with the same shaded gray ground. Each piece usually features a medallion or underglaze-painted Dickens character or scene under a glossy overglaze. Few well-done, artist-signed examples can be found, but it is still collectible based on its rarity.

Mug, Dickensware I, with squeezebag decoration and the inscription, "A Chirping Cupis My Matin Song," in green, brown, and white against a powder blue ground, artist's initials, 5" x 3-3/4", **$350-$500**.

Vase, Dickensware II, ovoid, decorated by J. H. with a woman playing a mandolin on a crescent moon, impressed mark, 8-1/2", **$500-$700**.

Vase, Dickensware III, bell-shaped, painted with figure of a man, "Mr. Weller Sr," signed and stamped, 8-1/4" x 7-1/4", **$750-$1,000**.

DRESDEN

The Dresden line, sometimes referred to as Holland, was introduced sometime between 1905 and 1910. The medium blue background is decorated in muted tones of blue and white slip with Dutch scenes. It is not a pattern that has caught on with collectors, although it is rare and most pieces are sizeable. Given its rarity, a surge in value seems inevitable; unfortunately, the pieces are often cracked, with most of them being utilitarian, and large pieces being prone to cracks in general.

It is very similar in decoration and technique to the Delta line. This line is rare and not clearly marked, so there is definitely some confusion as to which pieces are truly Delta. Many pieces believed to be from the Delta line are decorated with sailboats, Dutch scenes, and floral patterns on subdued shaded grounds.

Vase, Dresden, tall cylindrical, painted by Levi Burgess with a panoramic Delft scene, signed LJB, stamped Weller Matt, 16" x 4-1/2", **$500-$750**.

COLLECTOR TIP

While no one can accurately predict the future of the Weller market, several factors such as size, form and decoration can contribute to the value and desirability of a piece.

Sometimes marked Eosian, Eocean was produced from 1898 through sometime between 1915-1918. It is most often found with a shaded gray background, the underglaze decoration hand-painted on a white body. On rare occasion, you will find a piece in shades of pink, green, blue, or yellow.

There are numerous variations of this line, the earliest in softer tones, and later additions with a streaked black and blue background, commonly referred to as Late Eocean. Most pieces in this later line are bud vase forms, although larger pieces can be found. Even the best of the late pieces are coarsely decorated, and tend to be lower in value than the standard Eocean line.

Eocean Rose is yet another variation of the line, featuring the typical shaded gray ground with a very slight pink tint at the lightest end. It is sometimes very difficult to pick up on this trace of pink, but they can often be identified by "Rose" etched on the bottom.

While the standard gray background may be more desirable than the deep brown of Louwelsa, Eocean's artwork is usually far less refined. Many of the lesser Eocean forms hold little potential to gain much value, but the highly decorated, artist signed pieces are quickly finding their place in the finest of collections.

Jardinière, Eocean, pink carnations, unmarked, 7" x 8-1/2", **$150-$250**.

Vase, Eocean, bulbous, painted with cherries, impressed and incised marks, 5" x 5", **$150-$200**.

Vase, Eocean, bulbous, painted with red and white dogwood, impressed and incised marks, 6-1/2" x 4-3/4", **$300-$400**.

Vase, Eocean, flat shoulder and cupped rim, painted with red berries and leaves, incised mark, 7-1/4" x 5-1/4", **$350-$500**.

Vase, Eocean, with buttressed neck, painted with pink poppies in full bloom, a rare form, impressed mark, 8", **$750-$1,000**.

EOCEAN

Vase, Eocean, cylindrical, painted with pansies in purple, ivory, and brown, incised mark, 8" x 2-1/2", **$300-$400**.

Vase, Eocean, bulbous, painted with red berries and leaves, impressed mark, 8-1/2" x 5", **$350-$500**.

Vase, Eocean, ovoid, painted with dogwood, incised mark and unknown artist's mark, 9-1/2" x 4-1/4", **$500-$700**.

Vase, Eocean, bulbous, painted by Elizabeth Blake with a portrait of a kitten, incised mark and artist's signature, 8" x 4-1/4", **$1,500-$2,000**.

Vase, Eocean, cylindrical, painted with a bulldog, with ovoid inset details near the rim, marked, 10", **$1,500-$2,000**.

Vase, Eocean, squat base and long flaring neck, painted by Mae Timberlake with cherries, etched mark and artist's initials, 10-1/4" x 4", **$400-$600**.

Vase, Eocean, ovoid, painted with gooseberries and leaves, incised mark, 10-1/2" x 3-3/4", **$400-$600**.

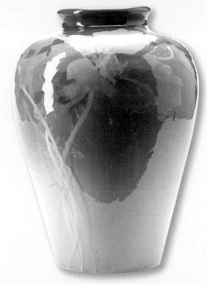

Vase, Eocean, finely painted by Levi Burgess with large pink poppies on an unusual shaded pink ground, incised mark and artist's initials, 10-1/2" x 7-1/2", **$1,000-$1,500**.

Pillow vase, Eocean, finely painted by Charles Chilcote with flying storks, marked in script artist's signature, 10-1/2" x 6-1/4", **$2,000-$3,000**.

Vase, Eocean, bulbous, finely painted by Levi Burgess with pink wild roses, impressed mark/L.J.B., 11-3/4" x 4-3/4", **$800-$1,200**.

EOCEAN

Vase, Eocean, painted with grapevines on a pale shaded gray-green ground, incised mark, 11-3/4" x 6-1/2", **$750-$1,250**.

Vase, Eocean, finely painted with purple sweet peas on a teal to gray shaded ground, incised mark, 12", **$650-$950**.

Vase, Eocean, bulbous, painted with deep pink Clematis, incised mark, 13-1/4" x 7-1/2", **$500-$700**.

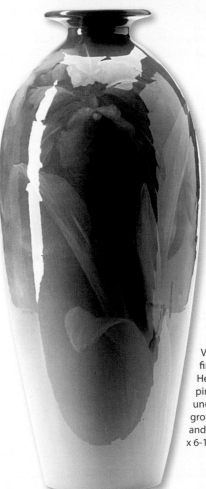

Vase, Eocean, tall, finely painted by Hester Pillsbury with pink orchids on an unusual shaded pink ground, incised mark and artist's mark, 15-1/2" x 6-1/2", **$2,000-$3,000**.

Vase, Eocean, tall, cylindrical, beautifully painted by Eugene Roberts with pink and ivory thistle, incised mark, 20-1/2" x 5-3/4", **$2,500-$3,000**.

Vase, Eocean or "gray on gray" Hudson-type, painted by Mae Timberlake with hydrangea on a pale shaded gray ground, marked with artist's signature, 16-1/2", **$1,500-$2,500**.

Vase, Eocean, ovoid, finely painted with flying birds, incised marks, 12", **$2,000-$3,000**.

Two pieces: a Late Eocean bud vase painted with a nasturtium, and an Etna pitcher painted with a purple pansy, one marked; bud vase: 5-1/4", **$100-$200**; pitcher: 6-1/4", **$75-$150**.

EOCEAN

Vase, Late Eocean, ovoid, painted with cherries, impressed mark, 9" x 4", **$250-$350**.

Three Late Eocean pieces: a small bulbous vase with colorful flowers and two four-sided tapered vases painted with cherries, unmarked; tallest is 6-1/2", **$50-$100** and the other two pieces are **$75-$125 each**.

Vase, Late Eocean, small, tapered, painted with daisies, impressed mark, 3-1/4" x 3", **$100-$200**.

Vase, Late Eocean, cylindrical, painted with berries and leaves, impressed mark, 9-3/4" x 4-1/4", **$250-$350**.

Two Late Eocean pieces: a flaring vase painted with lily-of-the-valley, and a tapering bud vase with cherries, one with impressed mark; flaring vase: 7-1/2", **$75-$150**; bud vase: 5-1/2", **$50-$100**.

Vase, Late Eocean, baluster, painted with pink and white chrysanthemums, unmarked, 11", **$250-$350**.

The Floretta line was introduced in 1904 and is decorated in relief with flowers and fruit in shades of brown, red, gray, and green. This pattern is similar to some forms included in the later Etna line, with the raised decorations created in the mold. The background, glazed in either glossy dark brown or gray to brown, sets the Floretta line apart from Etna. Very little artistry is involved in the production; the only hand-decoration is in painting the molded designs.

An Etna tapering vase with cherries, and a Floretta mug with a pink flower, both similar in coloring and decoration, but the Floretta has a hint of brown in the shaded background; both bear impressed marks; the vase is 9-1/2" and the mug is 5-1/4", **$50-$100 each**.

Vase, Floretta, three-sided with grapes, impressed mark, 7" x 3-1/2", **$100-$150**.

Vase, Floretta, cylindrical, with clusters of grapes, impressed mark, 9" x 3-1/4", **$50-$100**.

Vase, Floretta, large, bulbous, decorated with clusters of grapes, impressed Floretta mark, 12" x 8", **$200-$300**.

ETCHED FLORAL OR MODELED ETCHED MATT

Produced in 1910, Etched Floral or Modeled Etched Matt is a Frank Ferrell-designed line, the rarest pieces of which are hand incised by an artist, although most are molded. Though only the hand-incised pieces are usually found marked "Ferrell," his style of design is unmistakable.

Jardinière, Etched Floral or Modeled Etched Matt, decorated with grapevines, unmarked, 7" x 9", **$200-$300**.

Jardinière, Etched Floral or Modeled Etched Matt, by Frank Ferrell with sunflowers in burnt orange on ivory over celadon ground, artist's signature, 10" x 13-1/2", **$450-$650**.

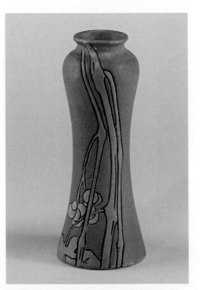

Vase, Etched Floral or Modeled Etched Matt, corseted, decorated with branches of berries and leaves on an orange ground, impressed mark, 10-3/4" x 4", **$350-$450**.

Vase, Etched Floral or Modeled Etched Matt, bulbous, decorated with yellow roses on an orange ground, impressed mark, 6-1/2" x 4-3/4", **$350-$450**.

ETCHED FLORAL OR MODELED ETCHED MATT

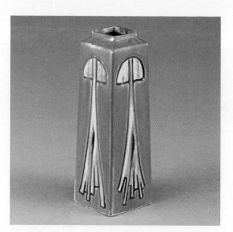

Vase, Etched Floral or Modeled Etched Matt, four sided with raised rim carved with mushrooms in white on an orange ground, impressed mark, 7", **$300-$400**.

Vase, Etched Floral or Modeled Etched Matt, four-sided, carved and painted with red and yellow tulips on an ivory ground, impressed mark, 8", **$300-$400**.

Vase, Etched Floral or Modeled Etched Matt, corseted, with berries, branches, and leaves on an ochre matt ground, unmarked, 13" x 4", **$350-$500**.

ETCHED MATT

Etched Matt was introduced in 1905; I am unsure as to when production ended. The glaze varies from a bisque-like matte glaze to a semi-gloss. The bodies are decorated with the face of a woman, and on most pieces her long, wavy blonde hair flows behind her, all on a medium green to pale brown ground. The Etched Matt line offers little variety of form and design, but sells well based on its rarity.

ETNA

Introduced in 1906, Etna is considered to be one of the last art ware lines produced for many years. Calling this line art ware is a bit of a stretch, because, along with Floretta, very little hand-decoration was involved in the production. Slightly more valuable examples with medallions of Shakespeare and other figures can be found, although they seem to fit more appropriately with the later Cameo Jewell line.

Jardinière and pedestal set, Etna, painted with pink nasturtium, unmarked, 25-1/2", **$750-$1,000**.

Vase, Etna, corseted, decorated with stemmed pink flowers, impressed mark, 4-1/2" x 3-3/4", **$150-$250**.

Vase, Etna, beaker-shaped, painted with pink flowers, impressed mark, 6" x 4-3/4", **$200-$300**.

Vase, Etna, gourd-shaped, painted with pink flowers, impressed Etna mark, 6-1/2" x 5-1/4", **$150-$250**.

Vase, Etna, ovoid, painted with purple flowers, unmarked, 7" x 3-3/4", **$200-$300**.

Vase, Etna, classically shaped, with pink roses, impressed mark, 10-1/4" x 4", **$250-$350**.

Vase, Etna, painted with tall daffodils, signed Weller on body and incised mark to base, 11-1/4" x 4-1/2", **$350-$450**.

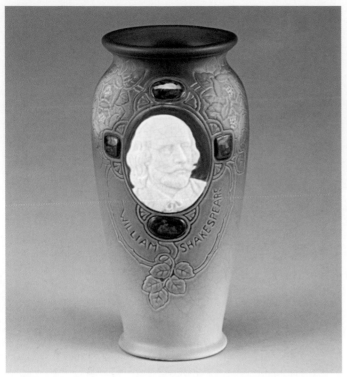

Vase, Etna, embossed with a portrait of Shakespeare and several jeweled accents, incised mark, 12", **$800-$1,200**.

Vase, Etna, ovoid with pink roses, impressed mark and signed on body, 14" x 9-1/4", **$400-$600**.

Vessel, Etna, squat, has two crossed handles, decorated with pink blossoms, impressed mark, 4-3/4" x 8-3/4", **$250-$350**.

The Fru Russet line was produced sometime around 1905 and the glazes were heavily curdled in a variety of colors. Buyers are never disappointed by the unusual forms and designs this line has to offer, and have made it one of the most highly sought after Weller patterns.

Weller Matt, which was probably produced around the same time, often shares shapes with Fru Russet, although it is covered in a rich matt glaze rather than mottled glazes.

One rare line, Reticulated, is often confused with the Fru Russet line because of its similar thick curdled glaze. Few examples from this line are known, but can be told apart by the reticulated, or cut-out designs.

Bowl, Fru Russett, squat, with berries and leaves on a blue ground, 6-1/2" diameter, **$500-$700**.

Pitcher, Fru Russett, lizard, deep rose, 5", **$950-$1,450**.

Bud vase or candle holder, Fru Russet, with tall red and yellow irises, impressed mark, 8-3/4" x 3-1/2", **$1,000-$1,500**.

Vase, Fru Russet, squat, decorated with white blossoms and leaves on one side, blue berries and leaves on the other, all on a mottled green ground, impressed mark, 3-1/2" x 5-1/2", **$1,000-$1,500**.

Vase, Fru Russet, squat, painted with flowers and berries on each side, 3-1/2", **$750-$1,000**.

Vase, Fru Russet, tapered, embossed with brown scarabs and red acanthus leaves on a blue and green ground, incised mark, 5" x 4-3/4", **$2,000-$3,000**.

Vase, Matt, bulbous, embossed with leaves under a deep rose matt glaze, impressed mark, 6" x 4-3/4", **$400-$600**.

Vase, Fru Russet, embossed with a salamander and covered in raspberry matte glaze, impressed mark, 4-3/4" x 3", **$1,000-$1,500**.

Vase, Fru Russet, gourd shaped, two handles, embossed with green leaves on a blue and rose ground, impressed mark, 6" x 6", **$1,000-$1,500**.

Three vases: two Fru Russet, one with chestnuts and one bud vase with two small handles, and a Kenova vase with a lizard perched on a strawberry plant, varied marks, 6-1/4" x 5", 9-1/2", **$750-$1,250, $650-$950**, and **$300-$400**.

FRU RUSSET/WELLER MATT

Vase, Fru Russet, thick curdled glaze, impressed numbers on bottom, 7-1/2", **$500-$750**.

Vase, Fru Russet, embossed with a bat and full moon hidden behind clouds, incised mark on body and impressed mark to underside, 8-1/2" x 7-1/2", **$2,000-$3,000**.

Vase, Fru Russet, green, two-handled, decorated with yellow wisteria blossoms, impressed WELLER, 7" x 5-1/2", **$750-$1,000**.

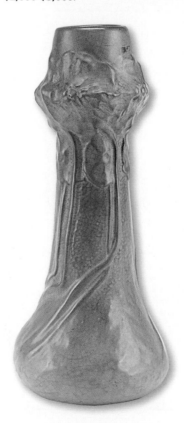

Vase, Fru Russet, embossed with tall flowers under a pale blue-gray and green glaze, impressed mark, 14" x 5-3/4", **$2,000-$3,000**.

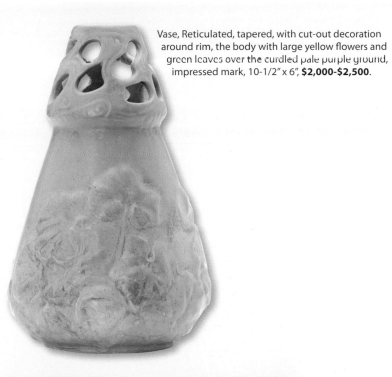

Vase, Reticulated, tapered, with cut-out decoration around rim, the body with large yellow flowers and green leaves over the curdled pale purple ground, impressed mark, 10-1/2" x 6", **$2,000-$2,500**.

Vase, Fru Russet, bulbous, exceptionally decorated by Pickens with pink lilies on a heavily curdled pale green ground, 13", **$3,000-$4,000**.

Vase, Fru Russet, embossed with wheat under a heavily curdled green and ivory glaze, impressed mark, 10-1/2", **$900-$1,400**.

FUDZI

Fudzi was created by Gazo Fujiyama in 1903 or 1904 with his entirely unique style; each piece is decorated with a woodland design. It is hard to distinguish these from similar lines he produced at Roseville, but the shapes can help you determine which is which. Also, Roseville will usually bear a seal or mark, whereas Weller's Fudzi line is mostly unmarked.

Vase, Fudzi, corseted, decorated with sunflowers, one of the very few known marked examples of this line, impressed mark, 8-1/2", **$1,000-$1,500**.

Vase, Fudzi, ovoid, leaves and berries around the rim, impressed numbers, 10-1/2", **$1,500-$2,000**.

Greenaways was introduced sometime before 1910. Much like the Dresden line, it is decorated with simple Dutch landscapes, although Greenaways is glazed in muted tones of green and yellow rather than blue. There is interest in this line because of its rarity and the many large pieces to be found, although the decoration rarely differs from one piece to the next. Much like the Etched Matt line, the greatest differences are in the forms themselves.

Hunter came to the market in 1904 and can be confused with the second Dickensware line. It is distinguished by its glossy dark caramel to deep chocolate brown glaze, and with incised decoration, most commonly ducks, and on rare occasion, seagulls.

Pillow vase, Hunter, painted with butterflies, incised mark and artist's initials, 5-1/4", **$350-$500**.

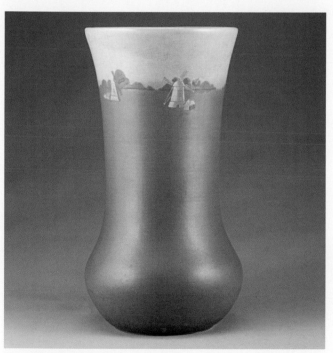

Floor vase or umbrella stand, Greenaways, incised S. A. Weller, 22", **$1,500-$2,500**.

Vase, Hunter, rare, slightly flared, incised with seagulls flying over waves, marked with impressed numbers, 7-1/4" x 3", **$600-$900**.

JAP BIRDIMAL AND RHEAD FAIENCE

The Jap Birdimal and Rhead Faience lines were designed by Frederick Hurten Rhead in 1903, after he left Vance Avon Pottery. The pieces he created at Avon, along with the new lines he designed with Weller and his similarly decorated Roseville Decorated Landscape line, are often confused for one another as they all display Rhead's signature squeezebag decorating methods.

His Jap Birdimal line was named for its Japanese influence, along with a combination of the words "bird" and "animal." Frequently it is decorated with geishas, birds, and the "bubble" trees very typical of Rhead's work.

Ewer, Jap Birdimal, finely decorated by Rhead with trees and a geisha, incised Weller Faience Rhead G580, 10-3/4" x 7", **$1,000-$1,500**.

Hair receiver, Jap Birdimal, closed-in rim, painted by Hattie Ross with Viking ships, artist's initials, 2" x 4", **$450-$650**.

Hair receiver, Jap Birdimal, decorated with Viking ships, 2" x 4", **$400-$600**.

Vase, Jap Birdimal, matte green, decorated with circular red and yellow flowers, unmarked, 4" x 5", **$800-$1,200**.

Vase, Jap Birdimal, star shaped, squat, flying white geese on a teal green and brown ground, impressed mark, 4-1/4" x 6", **$750-$1,000**.

JAP BIRDIMAL AND RHEAD FAIENCE

Vase, Jap Birdimal, tapered, has swimming fish, marked with artist's initials UNH, 6-1/4" x 3-1/4", **$800-$1,200**.

Vase, Jap Birdimal, three handles, bulbous, decorated in squeezebag with stylized green, brown, and white trees on a teal blue ground, incised Weller Faience E500-1/2, artist signed OMN, 8-1/4" x 5-1/2", **$1,500-$2,000**.

Roseville Decorated Landscape planter decorated in squeezebag with trees and geese around the rim, and four loop handles. These are often confused for Weller's Jap Birdimal line, but it was actually a line designed by Rhead while at Roseville, 5-1/2" x 7-1/4", **$500-$650**.

Vase, Jap Birdimal, tapered, decorated with a geisha against a burnt orange ground, a crisply decorated and well articulated example of this line, artist-signed CMM, an unidentified artist whose initials are often found on Jap Birdimal pieces, 7-1/2" x 3", **$1,000-$1,500**.

JAP BIRDIMAL AND RHEAD FAIENCE

One variation of the Jap Birdimal line features molded and painted tall dark blue trees on a shaded ivory and blue ground. While still considered to be a part of the Jap Birdimal line, less artistry is utilized and their lower values reflect this.

Jardinière, Jap Birdimal, with cobalt trees under a full moon on a light blue ground, impressed mark, 11-1/2" x 13-1/2", **$450-$650**.

Pedestal, Jap Birdimal, with cobalt trees against a line blue ground, unmarked, 16-1/2", **$500-$750**.

JAP BIRDIMAL AND RHEAD FAIENCE

The Rhead Faience line is most often simply decorated with landscapes, birds, or flowers. Rhead's decorating style is appealing to collectors of both Zanesville pottery, and to those collecting ceramics with strong Arts & Crafts influences. All of his lines rank among the most desirable in today's Weller market.

Teapot, Rhead Faience, decorated by L. P. with a panoramic village landscape in indigo on a blue-green ground, embossed Weller 3047/artist's initials, label from White Pillars museum, 5-3/4" x 9", **$800-$1,200**.

Three-piece set including a tea or coffee pot, creamer, and sugar bowl, Rhead Faience, each decorated in indigo squeezebag with windmills in a landscape on a teal blue ground, signed Rhead on body, pot 6-3/4", **$1,000-$2,000**.

Vase, Rhead Faience, bulbous, three-handled, painted with orange poppies on an olive ground, impressed 509, 8" x 7", **$1,250-$1,750**.

JAP BIRDIMAL AND RHEAD FAIENCE

Vase, Rhead Faience, bulbous, decorated in squeezebag with a band of walking ducks, and a geometric band around the rim, marked "Weller Rhead Faience", 8-3/4" x 6-1/4", **$2,500-$3,000.**

Vase, Rhead Faience, yellow, handled, with a band of ducks, signed Weller Faience with impressed numbers B500, 500, full Rhead signature which often indicates he decorated the piece himself, 8-1/2", **$2,000-$3,000.**

Vase, Rhead Faience, ovoid, blue with birds, signed Weller Faience with numbers, 11", **$3,000-$5,000.**

L'Art Nouveau, produced from 1903-1904, was also designed by Frederick Rhead and offered interesting Nouveau forms under simple bisque-like matt glazes. Occasionally they are found in a glossy glaze, which is usually only slightly more valuable than the matt. Most are floral, some with maidens, seashells, or woodland decoration. They are prone to having tight hairlines around the rim or underside of base, and if they are minor, will detract very little value. The more common, smaller forms in this line are not tremendously valuable, but the larger, rarer pieces have been a solid seller in the Weller market for many years.

Vase, L'Art Nouveau, with orange flowers and flowing leaves, 8-3/4", **$350-$500**.

Vase, L'Art Nouveau, four-sided, with panels of poppies and grapes, unmarked, 11" x 3-1/4", **$450-$650**.

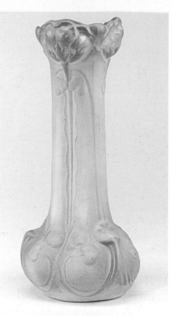

Vase, L'Art Nouveau, bottle-shaped, orange flowers and spade-shaped leaves, unmarked, 13" x 5", **$500-$700**.

Vase, L'Art Nouveau, shell-shaped, painted with maidens and flowers, impressed mark, 10" x 8-3/4", **$500-$700**.

Vessel, L'Art Nouveau, squat, nude woman wrapped around the rim, unmarked, 4", **$650-$950**.

LOUWELSA — 1896-1924

Samuel Weller began production in Zanesville after moving in 1888 from a small workshop in Fultonham, Ohio, where he had successfully created a market for painted flower pots and other utilitarian items. He then merged briefly in 1895 with William Long of the Lonhuda Faience Company, who brought along his company's dark blended-glaze techniques.

Cabinet vase, Lonhuda, classically shaped, painted by Albert Haubrich with delicate yellow blossoms on a green shaded ground, stamped mark and artist's initials, 5-1/4", **$300-$400**.

Vase, Lonhuda, three-footed, painted with gooseberries, impressed mark, 4-3/4", **$150-$250**.

Vessel, Lonhuda, squat, painted with a brown tulip, stamped mark, 4-3/4", **$200-$300**.

Weller soon began a pattern of brief mergers, quickly parting ways, it seems, only after obtaining glaze techniques and secrets from his fellow potters. Perhaps this is why Jacques Sicard and Henri Gellie were so guarded with their work on the Sicardo line, fully aware that they would become expendable should they divulge their glaze secrets to Weller.

Quickly splitting from Lonhuda in 1896, Weller continued producing this brown-glazed pottery under the name Louwelsa, offering approximately 500 different shapes and sizes. Examples of the Louwelsa line can also be found in shades of red or blue, in matt glazes, and silver overlay, which is some of the most rare. Weller successfully produced this line through 1924.

Vase, Louwelsa, blue, ovoid, painted with delicate bluish blossoms, 8-1/2" x 3-3/4", **$850-$1,250**.

Aladdin lamp-form clock, Louwelsa, rare, painted with flowers, impressed Louwelsa mark, 8-3/4" x 8-1/4", **$600-$800**.

With the variety of sizes and shapes available, and the length of production, it is safe to assume that Louwelsa is easy to come by. With such a large supply of pottery available, there is a lack of high demand. You would benefit from focusing on only the best examples. Look for sharper, more detailed work, lighter, nicely shaded backgrounds, and artist signatures. Portraits hold the most interest to collectors, with garden flowers being the most common, and least valuable. Certain Louwelsa artists are more highly regarded; some of the most popular are Levi Burgess, Hester Pillsbury, Anthony Dunlavy, Charles Dibowski, and Frank Ferrell.

Clock, Louwelsa, painted with yellow lilies, signed with artist's initials, 6", **$300-$500**.

Charles Upjohn joined the company in 1895, while the production of Louwelsa was still going strong. Although production of the Louwelsa line was very successful, Weller knew that buyers would soon demand something different, and the other companies in the Ohio River valley would be happy to fill any voids he left in the market. Upjohn quickly had his first line at Weller ready to offer to the public in 1897, Dickensware I.

Three Louwelsa pieces: a mug painted by Helen Windle with a cherry, 4-1/2", **$100-$200**; a chamberstick painted with cherry blossoms, 5", **$75-$150**; and a jug painted with berries, 5-1/2", **$150-$250**.

LOUWELSA — 1896-1924

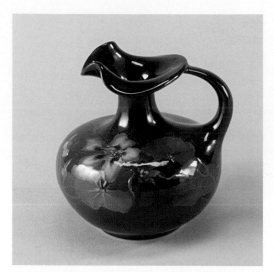

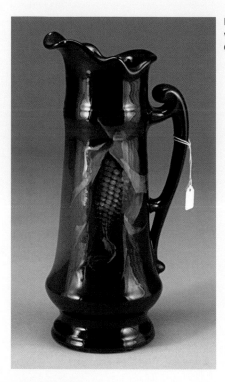

Ewer, Louwelsa, tall, painted by Madge Hurst with an ear of corn, impressed mark, 13-1/2" x 6-1/2", **$450-$650**.

Ewer, Louwelsa, squat, ruffled rim, painted with gold and brown nasturtium, impressed mark, 6-1/2" x 5-1/2", **$175-$275**.

Ewer, Louwelsa, squat, painted with a rose, impressed mark, 4-1/2" x 5-1/2", **$200-$300**.

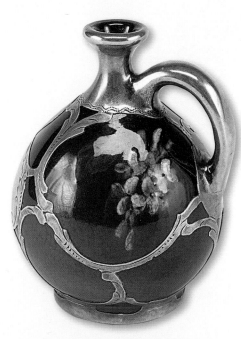

Jardinière, Louwelsa, painted with orange roses, impressed mark, 10" x 12-1/2", **$200-$350**.

Fine cabinet jug, Louwelsa, painted with small yellow blossoms, overlaid with silver, impressed mark, 3-3/4" x 2-3/4", **$1,000-$1,500**.

Jug, Louwelsa, squat, painted with oak branches, impressed mark, 3-1/4" x 5-3/4", **$150-$250**.

Jug, Louwelsa, ruffled rim, painted with yellow flowers, impressed mark, 6" x 5", **$150-$250**.

Jug, Louwelsa, painted by Minnie Mitchell with cherries, impressed mark and artist's initials, 6", **$150-$250**.

Two squat jugs or bud vases, Louwelsa, one painted with clover blossoms and the other with daffodil, both marked, 2-1/2" each, **$100-$200 each**.

Mug, Louwelsa, painted with a portrait of a man, impressed mark, 6-1/2" x 4-1/4", **$350-$500**.

Mug, Louwelsa, painted by J. E. with gooseberries and leaves, impressed Louwelsa mark and artist's initials, 6-1/4" x 5-1/2", **$150-$250**.

LOUWELSA — 1896-1924

Pedestal, Louwelsa, painted by Eugene Roberts with blackberries and branches, impressed mark and artist's initials, 23", **$300-$500**.

Oil lamp, Louwelsa, three-handled, footed, painted with berries, impressed mark. Pottery only: 7-1/4" x 10-3/4", **$300-$400**.

Pitcher and mug, Louwelsa, both painted with grapes, both marked, 12-1/2" and 6-1/2", **$150-$200** and **$200-$300**.

Floor vase, Louwelsa, painted by Lillie Mitchell with grape clusters, impressed mark and artist's signature, 18", **$750-$1,000**.

Floor vase, Louwelsa, rare, painted by E. Leffler with yellow roses on a shaded brown and lemon yellow ground, impressed mark and artist's signature, 28-1/4", **$4,000-$5,000**.

Pillow vase, Louwelsa, painted with wild roses, impressed mark, 4" x 5-1/4", **$100-$200**.

Vase, Louwelsa, gourd shaped, two handles, with gooseberry leaves, impressed mark, 5-1/2" x 4-1/2", **$100-$200**.

Pillow vase, Louwelsa, painted with orange poppies, unmarked, 5-1/2" x 5-1/2", **$150-$250**.

Vase, Louwelsa, painted with a yellow daffodil, impressed mark and artist's initials AC, 6-1/4" x 3-1/4", **$250-$350**.

Two Louwelsa vases: one corseted with nasturtium, the other bulbous and painted with pansies, impressed marks, 6" and 7", **$150-$250 each**.

Two Louwelsa pieces painted with flowers: a corseted vase, and a pitcher with ruffled rim, impressed marks, 7-1/4" each, **$200-$250** and **$150-$250**.

LOUWELSA — 1896-1924

Vase, Louwelsa, ovoid, painted with nasturtium, possibly by Ruth Axline, impressed mark and artist's cipher, 8-1/4" x 3-1/2", **$150-$250**.

Vase, Louwelsa, bulbous, painted by Elizabeth Blake with a Saint Bernard, stamped Louwelsa mark and artist's signature, 9-1/2" x 5-3/4", **$600-$800**.

Vase, Louwelsa, painted by Levi Burgess with a portrait of a Native American, 10-1/2" x 4", **$1,250-$1,750**.

Vase, Louwelsa, bulbous, painted with pansies, impressed mark, 9-1/2" x 3-3/4", **$150-$250**.

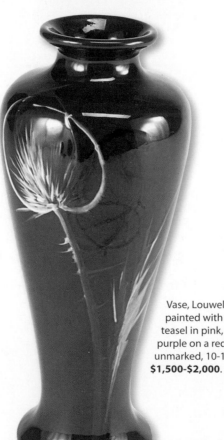

Vase, Louwelsa, red, painted with pink teasel in pink, ivory, and purple on a red ground, unmarked, 10-1/2" x 4", **$1,500-$2,000**.

Vase, Louwelsa, ovoid, painted with gooseberries and leaves, impressed mark, 10-1/2" x 5-1/2", **$150-$250**.

Vase, Louwelsa, bulbous, with lion medallions holding ring handles, painted by Albert Haubrich with palm fronds and banana leaves, stamped mark and artist's initials A.H., 10-3/4" x 10", **$600-$900**.

Vase, Louwelsa, blue, tall, ovoid, painted with branches of roses, impressed mark, 11" x 4", **$1,250-$1,750**.

Vase, Louwelsa, bulbous, painted by Lillie Mitchell with cherries, impressed mark and artist's initials, 11-1/2" x 7-1/2", **$300-$500**.

Vase, Louwelsa, bulbous, painted with orange and yellow carnations, impressed mark, 12" x 3-1/4", **$150-$250**.

LOUWELSA — 1896-1924

Vase, Louwelsa, bulbous, painted by Mae Timberlake with acorns and leaves, impressed mark and artist's initials, 13-1/2" x 6-1/4", **$250-$350**.

Vase, Louwelsa, large, bulbous, painted by Frank Ferrell with a vine of grapes, impressed and artist's mark, 12" x 8", **$500-$700**.

Vase, Louwelsa, corseted, painted with irises, impressed mark, 13" x 3-1/2", **$300-$500**.

Vase, Louwelsa, painted with yellow and orange chrysanthemums, impressed mark, 14" x 5", **$250-$350**.

Vase, Louwelsa, ovoid, finely painted by Levi Burgess with roses, impressed mark and artist's mark, 14-3/4" x 5", **$250-$450**.

Vase, Louwelsa, tall cylindrical, finely painted by Turner with a portrait of Napoleon, 18" x 5", **$1,250-$1,750**.

Vase, Louwelsa, large bulbous, painted by L. Blake with a basset hound, impressed Louwelsa mark and artist's signature, 15" x 12-1/4", **$1,000-$1,500**.

Vessel, Louwelsa, squat, painted with clover blossoms, possibly by Madge Hurst, impressed mark and illegible artist's mark, 3" x 5-1/2", **$100-$200**.

Vase, Louwelsa, large bulbous, finely painted with grapes, impressed mark, 16-1/4", **$400-$600**.

LOUWELSA — 1896-1924

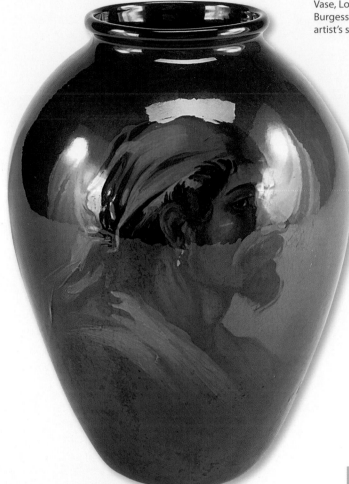

Vase, Louwelsa, large, bulbous, finely painted by Levi Burgess with a portrait of a pirate, stamped mark and artist's signature, 14", **$1,250-$1,750**.

Vessel, Louwelsa, squat, painted by A. S., with branches of wild roses, impressed mark, 3" x 5-1/2", **$150-$250**.

Vessel, Louwelsa, three-footed, painted with nasturtium, impressed Louwelsa mark, 6", **$150-$250**.

Water jug, Louwelsa, spherical, painted by Frank Ferrell with an ear of corn, impressed Louwelsa mark, 6-1/2" x 6-1/4", **$250-$350**.

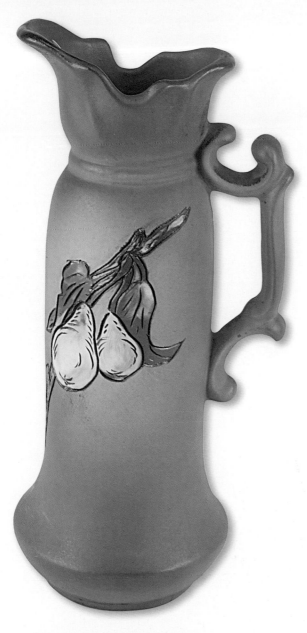

Matt Floretta was produced around 1904. Each piece is etched with fruit on a bisque ground. It could be easily mistaken for a Dickensware II piece, and it may even be a variation of that line, although you could say many of Weller's lines are variations on lines past. Much like Louwelsa, the value of Floretta has steadily fallen since the 1980s, with prices now falling slightly below similar Dickens II forms.

Ewer, Matt Floretta, incised with pears on a branch, incised mark, 10-1/2" x 4-1/2", **$250-$350**.

MATT GREEN

Blue bottom typically found on Weller's Matt Green pottery.

Matt Green was produced around 1905 and introduced some of the most interesting forms Weller had to offer. While it is said the Ohio pottery companies were not able to produce a green glaze as nice as that of Grueby Pottery, some of Weller's finest Matt Green pieces come close. The most desirable of all the Matt Green pieces are usually of architectural form or have reticulated or highly stylized designs. Nearly all of the pieces are unmarked and can be hard to identify, but can most often be distinguished by their blue-tinted bottoms.

This line has a very strong sales record, as it appeals to not only Weller buyers, but also to those collecting Arts & Crafts pottery.

Bowl, Matt Green, embossed with dragonflies, unmarked, 3-3/4" x 7-1/2", **$400-$600**.

Bowl, Matt Green, low, banded grapevine pattern, 9-1/4" diameter, **$500-$700**.

Three Matt Green pieces: an 8" candlestick with triangular base, a small vase with tapered neck, and a buttressed planter with impressed detail, one marked, **$350-$500, $300-$400**, and **$200-$300**.

Jardinière, Matt Green, closed-in rim, unmarked, 7-3/4" x 10-1/2", **$200-$300**.

Jardinière, Matt Green, embossed with Greek Key pattern and buttresses, unmarked, 8-1/4" x 10-1/2", **$350-$500.**

Jardinière, Matt Green, embossed, four handles styled as Arts & Crafts strap hardware, unmarked, 9-3/4" x 12", **$350-500.**

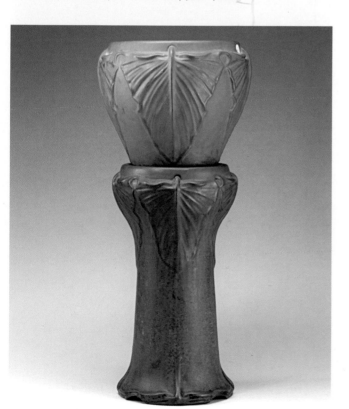

Jardinière and pedestal, Matt Green, not a set, embossed with broad leaves, unmarked, jardinière is 11-1/2" x 13", **$300-$400** and **$400-$600.**

Jardinière, Matt green, applied leaf handles, floriform feet, and embossed lilies, 15" x 15-1/2", **$750-$950.**

MATT GREEN

Vase, Matt Green, twisted, impressed mark, 5-1/4", **$400-$600**.

Lamp base, Matt Green, formed with twisted leaves at base and blossoms around the rim, unmarked, 14-1/2" x 6", **$1,500-$2,500**.

Planter, Matt Green, rare, architectural form, ribbed bands on body and buttressed handles, unmarked, 7" x 10", **$650-$950**.

Umbrella stand, Matte Green, embossed with geometric floral pattern, unmarked, 20" x 10", **$600-$800**.

Vase, Matt Green, with leaf-like design on the base and two angular handles, unmarked, 6-1/2", **$600-$1,000.**

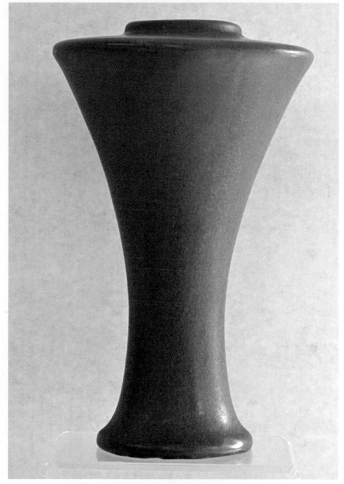

Vase, Matt Green, corseted, flat shoulder, this form is also seen in the Camelot line, unmarked, 11-1/2", **$850-$1,250.**

Vase, Silvertone, covered in a matt green glaze, 7", **$400-$500.**

MATT GREEN

Vase, Matt Green, tall, with banded handles, 12",
$1,500-$2,000.

Pair of vases, Matt Green, three-sided, embossed with tall flowers,
unmarked, 12-1/4" x 5", **$500-$700 each**.

Vase, Matt Green, corseted with reticulated rim and embossed poppy decoration, unmarked, 12-1/4" x 6-1/2", **$1,500-$2,500**.

Vase, Matt Green, unusual, with a molded band of apples around the rim, unmarked, 12-1/4" x 7", **$1,200-$1,500**.

Vase, Matt Green, tall corseted with geometric design, unmarked, 15-1/2", **$300-$400**.

Vase, Matt Green, large thistle blossoms and leaves, unmarked, 13-1/2", **$800-$1,200**.

Vessel, Matt Green, squat, incised with Native American designs, impressed mark, 5" x 6", **$750-$950**.

PERFECTO AND MATT LOUWELSA

The Perfecto and Matt Louwelsa lines were produced around 1904. Because pieces can be found etched either Perfecto or Matt Louwelsa, it leads the majority of collectors to believe that they were produced as entirely separate lines. They are extremely similar in style and are nearly impossible to differentiate. Most of the pieces found marked Matt Louwelsa have been more heavily textured and are less refined than those marked Perfecto.

Very similar lines were produced by Owens and Roseville as well, but the marks and shapes set them apart from those of Weller.

While designs of this type were popular at one point, they are not nearly as saleable today.

Vase, Perfecto, ovoid, very finely painted by Albert Haubrech with chrysanthemums, on a matt green ground, unmarked, 14-1/2" x 4-1/2", **$2,000-$3,000.**

COLLECTOR TIP

Finely decorated, artist-signed pieces stand out from the others. Those with common decoration, such as grapes or wild roses, pale in comparison to those with bats, cats, or cabins. A Hudson vase signed by Pillsbury is far more saleable than a vase lacking the artist's signature. Only rarely will a truly exceptional example of art ware be found without the artist's cipher, or even better a full signature, so the mark is usually a good indication of decorative quality.

Also called Sicardo, Sicard was produced from 1902 until 1907 and created by Jacques Sicard and his assistant Henri Gellie. While at home in France, Sicard had studied at the studio of Clement Massier, where he learned to make Massier's signature nacreous glaze.

Sicard was a costly line to make, and probably turned little profit, but it did keep Weller at the top of the market. It seems that profit became secondary at times because the competition between pottery makers in the Ohio area was fierce.

A buyer could very easily find numerous examples of the same form with different decorations. For this reason, you should be careful to choose the best examples you can find. Look for crisp, clear, properly fired designs, nice forms, and signatures on the body.

In many cases, it is smart to build a collection of the best pieces you can find, even if some are damaged or repaired. But in the case of Sicard, which is difficult to restore, a buyer would be wise to shy away from any pieces with serious damage such as large chips, cracks, or those with poor repairs.

Bowl or ashtray, Sicard, circular, buttressed, decorated with clover blossoms, marked Weller on body, 2-1/2" x 6-1/2", **$450-$650**.

Candlestick, Sicard, with stars and butterflies decoration, marked on body, 6-1/2", **$600-$800**.

Jardinière, Sicard, large, decorated with sunflowers, marked in script, 10-1/2" x 12", **$2,000-$3,000**.

Lamp base or vase, Sicard, with heavy glaze drips and unusual sea life decoration, 15-1/2", **$2,000-$3,000**.

SICARD

Lamp base, Sicard, bulbous, floral decoration, 15-1/2", **$2,000-$3,000**.

Bud vase, Sicard, triangular opening, with stars and moons, marked on body, 4-1/2" x 2-3/4", **$450-$650**.

Bud vase, Sicard, decorated with flowers, marked on body, 5-1/4" x 2-1/2", **$400-$600**.

Cabinet vase, Sicard, four-sided, daisies, marked on body, 4-1/2" x 2-1/2", **$400-$600**.

Cabinet vase, Sicard, decorated with falling leaves, marked on body, 4-1/2" x 3", **$400-$600**.

Floor vase, Sicard, fine and large, extensively decorated with flowers and leaves, signed on body and dated 1902, 25" x 13", **$5,000-$7,500**.

SICARD

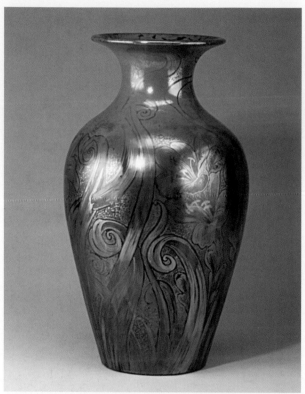

Vase with flowers, Sicard, bulbous, base is overfired in some areas, the top beautifully fired with excellent coloration, marked on body, 5-1/4" x 3-1/4", **$500-$700**.

Vase, Sicard, gourd shaped, with flowers and dots, marked on body, 3-3/4" x 3", **$400-$600**.

Floor vase, Sicard, fine and large, with lilies, marked on body, 26" x 15", **$5,000-$7,000**.

Vase, Sicard, gourd-shaped, faintly decorated with mums under a dripping glaze, no visible mark, 4-1/2" x 3", **$350-$450**.

Vase, Sicard, fine, squat, "blown-out" spade-shaped leaves and a perfectly fired glaze, 4-1/2", **$750-$1,000**.

Vase, Sicard, bulbous, with mistletoe, marked on body, 4-3/4" x 2-1/2", **$400-$600**.

Vase, Sicard, lobed, decorated with chrysanthemums, marked on body and impressed 38, 4-3/4" x 7", **$800-$1,200**.

Vase, Sicard, three-sided, with flowers and leaves, overfired around base, 5", **$350-$500**.

Vase, Sicard, twisted, decorated with clovers, very nicely fired, marked on body, 5" x 3", **$750-$950**.

Vase, Sicard, twisted, decorated with flowing lines, unmarked, 5" x 2-1/4", **$500-$750**.

SICARD

Vase, Sicard, tapered, has falling leaves, marked on body, 5" x 3-1/2", **$600-$900**.

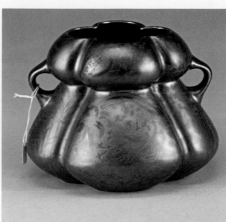

Vase, Sicard, gourd-shaped and painted with cornflowers in gold, perfectly fired, marked on body and impressed mark on bottom, 7-1/4", **$950-$1,250**.

Vase, Sicard, gourd shaped, with peacock feathers, perfectly fired, marked on body, 5-1/2" x 5", **$750-$1,000**.

Vase, Sicard, twisted, decorated with clovers, nicely fired, 5-1/2", **$800-$1,200**.

Vase, Sicard, corseted, decorated with foliage, overfired around base, 6-1/4", **$300-$400**.

Vase, Sicard, ovoid with sprays of flowers and leaves, unmarked, 7-3/4" x 2-1/2", **$400-$650**.

Vase, Sicard, gourd-shaped, with bold gold floral decoration on a bright purple ground, marked on body and impressed 41, 7-1/4" x 8", **$950-$1,250**.

Vase, Sicard, cylindrical, unusual "blown-out" irises and heavy glaze drips, 8", **$750-$1,000**.

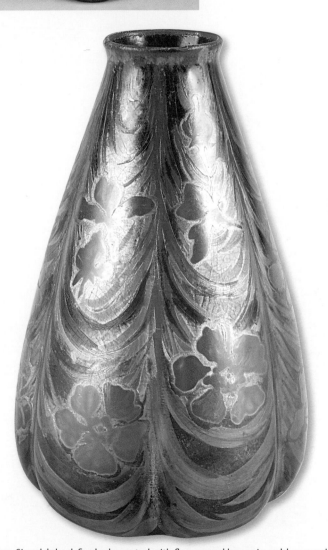

Vase, Sicard, lobed, finely decorated with flowers and leaves in gold on a red and purple ground, impressed 27, 8" x 5", **$1,500-$2,000**.

SICARD

Vase, Sicard, ovoid, decorated with berries and leaves, 8-1/2", **$750-$1,000**.

Vase, Sicard, ovoid, decorated with stylized chrysanthemums, marked on body, 9" x 5", **$750-$1,000**.

Vase, Sicard, decorated with thistle, exceptionally fired, no visible mark, 9-1/4" x 4", **$2,000-$3,000**.

Vase, Sicard, tapered, with tall ferns, no visible mark, 9", **$750-$1,000**.

Vase, Sicard, ovoid, with ruffled rim, decorated with blossoms and twisted leaves, marked on body, impressed on bottom, 9-1/2" x 3", **$800-$1,200**.

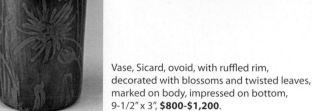

Vase, Sicard, tall, mistletoe decoration, the glaze very overfired around the base, marked on body, 10" x 3", **$600-$900**.

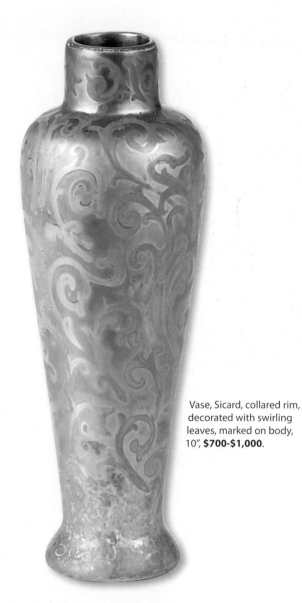

Vase, Sicard, collared rim, decorated with swirling leaves, marked on body, 10", **$700-$1,000**.

Vase, Sicard, decorated with chrysanthemums, marked on body, 10-1/2" x 5-1/2", **$1,250-$1,750**.

SICARD

Vase, Sicard, rare form, decorated with snails, nicely fired, marked on body, 10", **$1,750-$2,750**.

Vase, Sicard, rare bottle shape, decorated with pine branches, marked on body, 13-3/4" x 6-1/4", **$1,250-$1,750**.

Vase, Sicard, large bulbous with painted and modeled dandelions, marked on body, 15", **$3,500-$5,500**.

Vase, Sicard, decorated with thistle in gold against a purple, blue and green ground, 15-1/2" x 5-1/2", **$1,500-$2,000**.

Vase, Sicard, four-sided, decorated with holly and leaves, some overfiring near the base, marked on body, 16", **$1,250-$2,000**.

Vessel, Sicard, squat, decorated with gold berries and leaves, marked on body, 4-3/4" x 7-3/4", **$600-$800**.

TURADA

Henry Schmidt designed the company's first squeezebag line, "Turada," beginning production in 1897. Squeezebag, also known as slip trail or tube lining, is a raised decoration applied by squeezing glaze through a small hole in an instrument, much like decorating a cake. The highly detailed, often reticulated decoration on Turada became problematic, and production ended just the year after it began. It is perhaps overlooked because of the design's strong Victorian influences. It is a great value when you consider the amount of hand decoration involved in creating each piece. Turada vases are particularly valuable because nearly all examples are found fashioned as oil lamps, jardinières, mugs, and bowls.

When comparing the prices of similar squeezebag lines produced by Jervis, Roseville, and Arequipa, this line's potential to increase in value seems great.

Biscuit jar, Turada, with an ivory foliate decoration on an indigo ground, impressed Turada mark, #615, 6-3/4" x 5-1/2", **$250-$350.**

Bowl, Turada, corseted, impressed mark, 3-1/4" x 8", **$150-$250.**

Mug, Turada, twisted handle, Weller Turada mark, 6", **$75-$150.**

Jardinière, Turada, massive with banded floral decoration in orange and ivory on an olive ground, impressed Turada 217 mark, 17" x 18", **$1,000-$1,500.**

Oil lamp, Turada, three-footed, no visible mark, pottery is 7-3/4", **$450-$650**.

Oil lamp base, Turada , blue, coral, and ivory banded decoration on a dark green ground, impressed Turada 561 mark, pottery: 7-1/4" x 14", **$400-$600**.

Vessel, Turada, oil lamp-shaped, impressed mark, 6" x 9-1/2", **$350-$550**.

WELLER MATT WARE

Weller Matt Ware appears to be a variation of the L'Art Nouveau line, the same Nouveau form repeated in a flat green-blue glaze. It is not known if this is a separate line entirely, or simply a part of the Nouveau line with a different glaze color.

Vase, Weller Matt Ware, two-handled with swirled design, incised Matt Ware mark, 8-3/4" x 7", **$400-$600**.

COLLECTOR TIP

It is understandably difficult for those new to the Weller market to separate the run-of-the-mill decoration from the outstanding, but with a little research and experience, it becomes easy to divide the two.

Middle Period to Late Art Ware and Commercial Ware

In 1911, Weller's focus shifted to commercial ware, which proved to be a more profitable venture. The artist-decorated pieces were very time consuming, required far more manpower, and often didn't meet the high standards required to offer a piece for sale.

Rudolph Lorber had begun working with Weller in 1905, and he was soon put in charge of creating new lines through the mid-1930s. His innovative designs were unlike anything other companies in the area were producing at that time, making them popular both then and now.

Middle period to late art ware and commercial ware lines are listed alphabetically. For the chronological order of when these pottery lines were introduced, see Production Dates on Pages 15 and 16.

ANSONIA

Ansonia was produced in the late 1920s. The forms are practical, with ribbed bodies and very basic, muted, matt glazes in shades of orange and brown. This pattern is very difficult to find, and though it is very plain in its design, is highly valued among utilitarian wares.

Batter jug, Ansonia, covered in a mottled green and yellow glaze, signed Weller in script, 10" x 8", **$100-$200**.

COLLECTOR TIP

It is wise to get ahead of the trends in the ceramic market. While a piece may not be particularly desirable today, it may be tomorrow. If you purchase a currently underappreciated piece at its lowest price point, you'll often see the value rise as trends fluctuate.

ARDSLEY

Ardsley was produced from 1920 through 1928. The pieces are molded with irises, lily pads, and cattails glazed in blue, green, and white. The vase forms and large flaring bowls are of the most interest to buyers. The flaring bud vases, candlesticks, and double bud vases are most common and the least valuable of all the Ardsley forms.

Vase, Ardsley, flaring, with cattails and water lilies, stamped mark, 9" x 3-3/4", **$100-$200**.

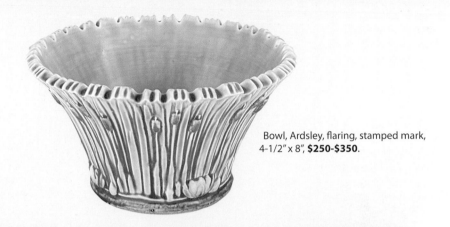

Bowl, Ardsley, flaring, stamped mark, 4-1/2" x 8", **$250-$350**.

Bowl and flower frog, Ardsley, bowl 14-1/2" l, **$350-$500**.

ARDSLEY

Vase, Ardsley, with stepped base, stamped mark, 10" x 5-1/4", **$300-$500**.

Double vase, Ardsley, with tall cattails, stamped mark, a particularly nice example, 10" x 9", **$200-$300**.

Large Ardsley flaring bowl and Kingfisher flower frog, stamped mark, 9-1/2" x 16" diameter, **$650-$950**. Both are fine examples of these forms.

Four Ardsley pieces: a double bud vase, a pair of candlesticks, and a flaring bud vase, 10", 3", 9", **$200-$300, $150-$250,** and **$100-$200**.

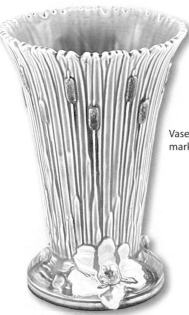

Vase, Ardsley, flaring, stamped mark, 10-1/2" x 7-1/2", **$250-$350**.

Vase, Ardsley, partitioned, unmarked, 10-1/2" x 6", **$300-$400**.

ATHENS

Produced around 1915, pieces in the Athens line are decorated with impressive mythological medallions or gargoyles. The backgrounds are also highly varied, sometimes glossy black, other times unglazed. It is highly sought after, but rarely found.

It is difficult to accurately place values on this line because the buyers' market is extremely competitive.

ATLAS

Produced from 1934 until the late 1930s, Atlas pieces are formed like three-dimensional shooting stars, with the interiors glazed in ivory and exteriors in pale apricot, yellow, or blue. A few forms even have designs molded in low-relief, and all bear impressed shape numbers on the underside.

The value of the Atlas line is minimal, topping out at around $300.

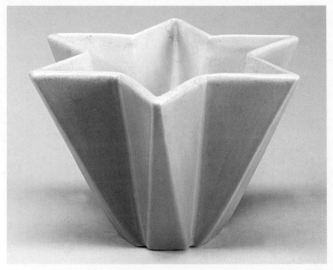

Vase, Atlas, flaring, in blue and ivory, script mark, 6" x 9-1/4", **$150-$250.**

Vase, Athens, with mythological medallions, 9-3/4" x 6", unmarked, **$750-$1,000.**

Vessel, Atlas, light yellow, bulbous, marked Weller C-3, 4" x 6", **$100-$200.**

Baldin was produced from 1915 through 1920, in both brown and blue. A more unusual variety can be found in glossy glaze, but it doesn't have any more value than the standard matt-glazed wares. The pattern itself doesn't differ greatly from piece to piece, nor is it that innovative, but has been consistently popular with buyers over the past five to ten years. Look for sharp details and bright colors, with few glaze flaws such as bursts or misses, which will increase its value.

Jardinière, Baldin, brown, impressed mark, 9" x 13", **$350-$550**.

Planter or bowl, Baldin, blue, unmarked, 4-1/4" x 8", **$200-$300**.

Jardinière and pedestal set, Baldin, impressed mark, 38" overall, **$1,000-$1,500**.

Planter or vase, Baldin, brown, squat, impressed mark, 5-3/4" x 6-3/4", **$150-$250**.

BALDIN

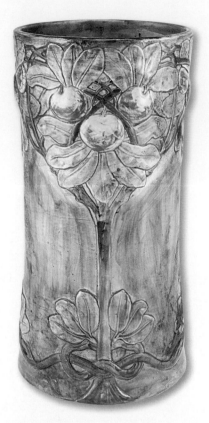

Umbrella stand, Baldin, brown, unmarked,
$1,000-$1,750.

Three brown Baldin pieces: a 6" planter and two bud vases, one 7" and one 8-1/2", one bears
impressed mark; planter, **$100-$200**; bud vases, **$150-$250 each**.

Two Baldin brown vases: one glossy 7", the other a 6" matte bud
vase, both have impressed marks, **$150-$250** and **$100-$200**.

Vase,
Baldin, blue,
bulbous,
unmarked,
7-1/4" x 6",
$150-$250.

Pair of vases, Baldin, bottle-shaped, one with pale decoration and one with apples in bright red glaze, impressed mark to one, 7-1/2" each, **$100-$200 each**.

Pair of vases, Baldin, corseted, one brown and one blue, unmarked, 9-1/2" x 5-1/2" each, **$300-$400 each**.

Vase, Baldin, brown, large, bulbous, two branch handles, impressed mark, 9-1/2" x 9", **$300-$500**.

Vase, Baldin, large, blue, bulbous, impressed mark, 9-1/2" x 9", **$400-$600**.

Vase, Baldin, brown, tapered, impressed mark, 13" x 7-1/2", **$450-$650**.

Vase, Baldin, blue, tapered, impressed mark, 13" x 7-1/2", **$500-$700**.

Two squat vessels, Baldin, one blue and one brown, one impressed mark, 5-3/4" x 6-3/4", **$150-$250 each**.

Vessel, Baldin, brown with a wide, squat body, 7" x 9", **$500-$700**.

BARCELONA

Introduced in the late 1920s, each Barcelona piece has a bright yellow glaze and painted floral design, reminiscent of European tourist ware. There is little variation and value in the Barcelona line.

Vase, Barcelona, tall corseted, buttressed handles, 14", unmarked, **$500-$750**.

Vase, Barcelona, bulbous, stamped mark, 11" x 6-1/4", **$250-$350**.

Vase, Barcelona, large baluster, stamped Barcelona Weller, Barcelonaware paper label, 11", **$300-$400**.

Jug, Barcelona, Barcelonaware label, 6-1/2" x 5-1/2", **$100-$200**.

BEDFORD GLOSSY AND BEDFORD MATT

Umbrella stand, Bedford Matt, covered in the standard matt green glaze, unmarked, 20" h, **$600-$900**.

The Bedford Glossy and Bedford Matt lines were produced in 1915. The forms are corseted, with flowers alternating between tall leaves. Examples are most commonly seen in a very deep green matt glaze, sometimes with charcoaling, with the glossy line in a streaked majolica-type glaze.

BESLINE

Besline, one of John Lessell's signature lines, was produced from 1920-1925. The lustered orange glaze is similar to that of the Lustre line, but it is decorated with flowers, berries, or leaves in white. Many of the Besline examples are prone to having wear to the orange overglaze, with bright white showing through. This will substantially detract from the value of the piece, unless it is minor and does not cover any of the decorated areas. Finding an example of Besline in perfect condition can be difficult, and the prices for which can be very competitive.

Pair of tall candlesticks, Besline, decorated with berries and leaves, unmarked, 11" h each, **$250-$350 pair**.

Vase, Besline, bulbous, decorated with berries and leaves on a lustred orange ground, unmarked, 8-1/2" x 6", **$350-$500**.

BLO' RED

Blo' Red was produced from the late 1920s until 1931. It is similar to the Chengtu line in glaze, but the Blo' Red glaze is deeper red with some mottling, rather than a solid matt orange.

Two bulbous vases: one Chengtu, the other Blo' Red, stamped marks, 3-3/4" h each, **$150-$200 each**.

Vase, Blo' Red, ovoid, covered in a bright orange mottled glaze, 9" x 4", **$200-$300**.

Blue Drapery was brought to market in 1915; each piece has a dark blue draped background and small pink floral accents. It has never been very popular with buyers, although the jardinière and pedestal sets draw considerable interest.

Three Blue Drapery pieces: 2" bowl, 3" bowl, and a 4-1/4" pillow vase, one with impressed mark, **$50-$100 each**.

Jardinière and pedestal set, Blue Drapery, unmarked, 29" overall, **$600-$900**.

Pair of candlesticks, Blue Drapery , stamped marks, 9-1/2" h, **$100-$200/pair**.

Wall pocket, Blue Drapery, 9", **$200-$300**.

BLUE AND DECORATED AND WHITE AND DECORATED

Both produced in the early 1920s, Blue and Decorated and White and Decorated are variations of the Hudson line. The background is either cream or deep blue, with a hand-painted decoration. In general, it is not favored by buyers, and nearly all of the pieces fall in the $100-$250 range. Banded floral designs are most common, particularly branches of cherry blossoms. Those with painted designs such as birds or feathers are high in value and difficult to find.

Vase, Weller Blue and Decorated Hudson, ovoid, painted with clusters of pink blossoms and bright green leaves, impressed mark, 8" x 5", **$150-$250**.

Vase, Blue and Decorated Hudson, tear-shaped, painted with white roses, impressed mark, 9", **$300-$400**.

Four vases, Blue and Decorated Hudson, each decorated with bands of colorful flowers, all marked, 9-3/4" and 8", **$150-$250 each**.

Three vases, Blue and Decorated Hudson, one faceted and two bulbous with cherry blossoms or roses, impressed marks, 10", 7-3/4", and 8-1/4", **$150-$250 each** and **$200-$300 each**.

Three vases, Blue and Decorated Hudson, two bulbous and one faceted, all marked, 10" and 8", **$200-$300** and **$150-$250**.

BLUE AND DECORATED AND WHITE AND DECORATED

Vase, White and Decorated, pear-shaped, painted with cherry blossoms, impressed mark, 7" x 4-1/4", **$200-$300**.

Vase, Blue and Decorated, tapering, painted with berries and leaves, impressed mark, 13-1/2" x 4-1/4", **$300-$500**.

Vase, Blue and Decorated, faceted, painted with a bluebird and cherry blossoms, impressed mark, 11-1/2" x 5", **$1,000-$1,500**.

Vase, Blue and Decorated Hudson, faceted, painted with a band of pink and white peonies, impressed mark, 11-1/2" x 5", **$250-$350**.

Three vases, White and Decorated Hudson, one squat with branches of cherry blossoms and unusual blended background, one four-sided with pink flowers on a blue trellis, and one faceted with pink and yellow wild roses around the rim, impressed marks, 4", 9-1/2", 7-3/4", **$150-$250 each**.

Vase, White and Decorated Hudson, painted with a band of roses around the rim, impressed mark, 7-1/2" x 4-1/4", **$100-$150**.

Two vases, White and Decorated, one painted with cherry blossoms, the other with chrysantemums, both have impressed mark, 7" x 8-1/2", **$200-$300** and **$150-$250**.

Two vases, White and Decorated, one ovoid painted with berries, the other with cherry blossoms, both marked, 8-1/2" and 10", **$250-$350** and **$150-$250**.

BLUE AND DECORATED AND WHITE AND DECORATED

Vase, White and Decorated Hudson, faceted, painted with bands and clusters of light and deep pink flowers, impressed mark, 11-1/4", **$300-$400**.

Vase, White & Decorated Hudson, tear-shaped, painted with berries and leaves on a cream ground, impressed mark, 8-3/4" x 4", **$200-$300**.

A variation of the Decorated Hudson lines on a gray ground, impressed mark, 9-3/4" x 5", **$350-$500**.

Three vases, White and Decorated Hudson, one squat, one faceted and one tear-shaped, all painted with branches of cherry blossoms, impressed marks, 8-3/4", 7-3/4", and 4", **$100-$200** and **$150-$250 each**.

Vase, White and Decorated
Hudson, classically shaped,
with branches of pink and
ivory roses, impressed mark,
13" x 6-1/2", **$600-$800**.

Vase, White and Decorated Hudson, tear
shaped, painted with blueberries, three
of the leaves sketched but not painted in,
impressed mark, 11-1/2", **$450-$650**.

Vase, White and Decorated Hudson,
classically shaped, with branches of deep
pink and ivory roses, 13" x 6-1/2", **$600-$800**.

Introduced prior to 1920, Blue Ware is often confused for the blue glazed ware of the Flemish line. The ground is blue as the name suggests, with each piece decorated with maidens and/or garlands of flowers. Both the jardinières and the vases are common. Consequently, they are less valuable than most of the wares produced in the early 1920s.

Planter, Blue Ware, footed, with maidens in yellow dresses, unmarked, 7-1/4" x 8", **$200-$300**.

Vase, Blue Ware, flaring, impressed mark, 8-3/4" x 4-1/2", **$200-$300**.

Vase, Blue Ware, ovoid, with maiden in yellow dress, impressed mark, 7-1/4" x 3-3/4", **$150-$250**.

Vase, Blue Ware, ovoid, features a maiden playing an instrument, unmarked, 8-1/2" x 3-1/2", **$150-$250**.

Vase, Blue Ware, large, has maidens dancing and playing instruments, stamped mark, 12" x 6-1/2", **$300-$400**.

BONITO

The Bonito line was introduced in 1927, continuing through 1933. Each piece is decorated with painted bands and floral designs, reminiscent of tourist wares, the ground accented with a sheer glaze over the clay. Most forms and designs are considered to be common, although some of the larger vases and wall pockets are hard to come by, and higher in value.

Bowl, Bonito, low, painted with swirled design and lily-of-the-valley, marked in script, 9-1/4" diameter, **$100-$200**.

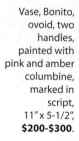

Vase, Bonito, bulbous, painted with pink daisies, marked in script, 6" x 5-1/4", **$75-$150**.

Vase, Bonito, bulbous, painted with tulips, marked in script, 7-1/2" x 4-1/2", **$100-$150**.

Vase, Bonito, flaring, painted with a blue flower and leaves, incised mark, 9-1/4" x 5-3/4", **$100-$200**.

Vase, Bonito, ovoid, two handles, painted with pink and amber columbine, marked in script, 11" x 5-1/2", **$200-$300**.

Wall pocket, Bonito, unmarked, 10-1/2" x 6", **$450-$650**.

Figure, pheasant, Brighton, unmarked, 5" x 7", **$400-$600**.

Brighton was produced in 1915. It is the glossy counterpart to Muskota; the pieces are bright and cheerful, and were ideal for gift-giving at the time. The line is composed of small figures, dishes, and flower frogs, along with large birds, most of which are very collectible and valuable. The large birds are nearly non-existent, or may go unrecognized because they were so rarely marked.

Parrot on a perch, Brighton, large size, impressed WELLER, 7-1/4" x 5-1/2", **$750-$1,000**.

Pair of colorful parakeets on a branch, Brighton, 9", **$950-$1,450**.

BRIGHTON

Two-duck flower frog, Brighton
(sometimes attributed to the
Muskota line),
5-1/2", **$300-$500**.

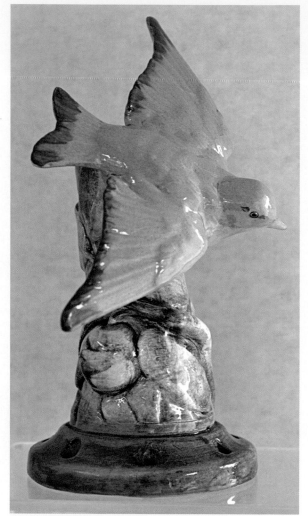

Flower frog, Brighton, flying blue bird and apple tree, unmarked,
9", **$750-$1,000**.

Flower frog, Brighton, with two swans, impressed mark, 6" x 9", **$500-$750**.

BRONZE WARE

Produced before 1920, Bronze Ware forms are often very large, with no shape being especially common. Each piece is covered in a heavily textured bronze-like glaze, some with a raised, curdled surface. The lamp base forms, though rare, bring only a fraction of what a vase would sell for.

Vase, Bronze Ware, ovoid, using a Drapery mold, covered in a bronze feathered glaze, stamped mark, 9-1/2" x 4-3/4", **$400-$600**.

Vase, Bronze Ware, tall, curdled reddish bronze glaze, unmarked, 13", **$600-$800**.

Baluster vase, Bronze Ware, tall, unmarked, 13-3/4" x 7", **$1,000-$1,500**.

BURNTWOOD AND ITS "SISTER-LINE" CLAYWOOD

Burntwood and its "sister-line" Claywood were first introduced by Lorber in 1910, both offering numerous examples in the Arts and Crafts style. They are nearly exact in design, although the Claywood line has bands separating the decoration into panels. These bands were most likely added to disguise the mold lines running down the sides of the body.

Both the Burntwood and Claywood lines are often stained, and are likely to have glaze flaking around the rim and base. Many of the forms are smaller cabinet pieces, with common decorations such as mice, fruit, and butterflies. Sometimes a very unusual example is found for sale, but rarely do they bring big money. The dollar value of these pieces may not be high individually, but it is fairly easy to put together a collection of the larger and more unusual forms that, as a whole, could attract the eye of even an advanced collector or dealer.

Teakwood was a later variation of this line, produced in 1915, far rarer than its predecessors.

Yet another variation was introduced at the same time, Dechiwo, with excised satyr design on brown ground. Examples from this line are nearly impossible to find, all with a high price tag.

Plate, Burntwood, large, decorated with swimming fish, unmarked, 12" diameter, **$450-$650.**

Vase, Burntwood, bulbous, with a band of flowers, unmarked, 3-3/4" x 4-1/4", **$100-$150.**

Jardinière, Burntwood, large, with roosters, impressed mark, 8-1/2" x 9-1/2", **$300-$400.**

BURNTWOOD AND ITS "SISTER-LINE" CLAYWOOD

Vase, Burntwood, cylindrical, crisply decorated with figures, unmarked, 8" x 4", **$300-$500**.

Two Burntwood pieces: a bulbous vase with morning glories, and a mug incised with "Wildey Picnic, Zanesville 1910," unmarked, 8-1/2" and 5", **$200-$300** and **$150-$200**.

Vase, cylindrical, Burntwood, decorated with Egyptian figures, paper label, 9-1/2", **$300-$400**.

Vase, Burntwood, bulbous with morning glories; this example shows a weak mold, unmarked, 8-1/2" x 6", **$200-$300**.

Two vases, Claywood, both with panels of flowers, unmarked, 2-1/2" x 3-1/4", **$150-$250 each**.

Vase, Claywood, flaring with butterflies, unmarked, 3" x 3-1/4", **$150-$200**.

Vase, Claywood, with swimming ducks, unmarked, 3" x 3-1/4", **$150-$200**.

BURNTWOOD AND ITS "SISTER-LINE" CLAYWOOD

Vase, Claywood, corseted, decorated with pinecones and needles, impressed mark, 6-1/2" x 4-1/4", **$150-$250**.

Vase, Clewell, metal covering a Weller Burntwood blank depicting a band of mythological figures, 8" x 4", **$600-$900**.

Vase, Claywood, faceted, with grapevines, impressed mark, 8-1/2" x 4", **$100-$200**.

Open vessel, Claywood, with fish, unmarked, 2" x 3", **$150-$250**.

Vase, Dechiwo, features satyrs dancing under vines, marked A. Lorber on the body, 13" x 7-1/2", **$3,000-$4,000**.

BUTTERFLIES, BIRDS, BUGS, AND BEES

Butterfly figure, sheer gray glaze with black dots, unmarked, 1" x 3-1/2", **$250-$450**.

Produced in 1915, butterflies, birds, bugs and bees pieces are very scarce. They come in a wide array of glazes and designs, from sheer gray to bright yellow. All are hard to find, even more so in mint condition. Perhaps due to their small size, the values have remained remarkably low.

Butterfly in brown and yellow, unmarked, 3" x 2", **$300-$500**.

COLLECTOR TIP

Large forms, 12 inches or taller, are more likely to retain or increase in value than the smaller examples. Large examples are far less common for several reasons: They were produced primarily for exhibitions, or to be given as presentation items, consuming a lot of the artist's time and attention. They were expensive even at that time, and were considered to be luxury items. Small pieces were manufactured in greater quantity because they utilized less artistry, making them less costly to produce.

CAMELOT

Camelot was produced in 1913. The background varies from yellow or orange, to olive green, all with stylized swirled designs in white. It is a very rare pattern, attracting competitive buyers seeking any and all forms. This line is prone to heavy crazing, which will deter only the most selective of buyers.

Dish, Camelot, yellow, footed, 8", **$500-$700.**

Vase, Camelot, corseted, gray-green and white, unmarked, 11-1/2", **$1,750-$2,750.**

Vase, Camelot, large and rare, unmarked, 12" x 5-1/2", **$2,000-$2,500.**

Vase, Camelot, large bulbous, yellow and white, unmarked, 8-1/2", **$1,500-$2,500.**

Cameo was produced from 1935 until the late 1930s. The backgrounds are a pale orange, green, or blue, with bold white floral designs. The latest of Weller's floral ware, it holds very little value to buyers, and is one of the most common lines Weller offered.

Two Cameo pieces: one blue and one orange, both marked in script, 7-1/2" and 5-1/4", **$75-$150** and **$50-$75**.

CAMEO JEWELL

Cameo Jewell was introduced in 1910. Some pieces can be found double-marked Etna, and the coloring and decorating styles are quite similar to each other. The Cameo Jewell line is most easily distinguished by the medallions with maidens, and figures, along with cabochons set into the body. Examples found without cameos, but ones that share the shaded gray ground and inset jewels, are still a part of the Cameo Jewell line. A later line, coined "Jewell" by collectors, also has jewels set into the body, but the background is a shaded yellow-brown.

Jardinière, Cameo Jewell, impressed mark, 7-1/2" x 10", **$300-$500**.

CAMEO JEWELL

Umbrella stand, Cameo Jewell, shaded gray ground, 22-1/2", **$750-$1,250**.

Umbrella stand, Cameo Jewell, impressed mark, 22-1/2", **$1,000-$2,000**.

Fine vase, Jewell, embossed with men and women around the rim above a jeweled band, impressed mark, 10-3/4" x 5-1/2", **$1,500-$2,000**.

Produced in the late 1920s, the background color on Chase pieces is most often found in deep blue with raised white hunting scenes, although variations can be found in several different colors and styles. One variation is found with silver overlay, another with silver painted designs on a dark ground. Although the standard pieces are rare, and the variations are extremely rare, they are not of great value.

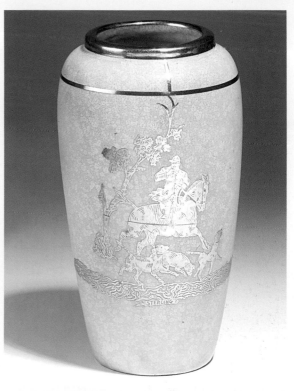

Vase, Chase, small, bulbous, incised mark, 5-1/2" x 5", **$200-$300**.

Vase, Chase, bulbous, marked in script, 8" x 5", **$300-$400**.

Vase, Chase-type, with silver appliqué on a seafoam green ground, 9", **$400-$600**.

CHENGTU

Chengtu was produced from 1925 through 1936. While the glaze and forms in the Chengtu line are basic and offer little variation, the interest in this line is stronger than the other undecorated, simply glazed forms.

Vase, Chengtu, faceted, stamped mark, 9-1/4" x 4", **$200-$300**.

CLAIRMONT

Clairmont was produced in 1920. It is a very unique line and the pieces are glazed in a dark brownish-red. The shapes are very different than all others produced by Weller. Their ribbed bodies give them the look of a hand-thrown piece, and many of the forms feature unusual curvy handles, and applied flowers. They are difficult to find, especially without damage.

CLASSIC

Produced from the early 1930s until 1935, Classic was made in soft tones of orange, ivory, blue, and green, the cut-out rim forming a trellis pattern. The forms are utilitarian yet soft and delicate in design.

CLINTON IVORY

Designed by Lorber, Clinton Ivory began production sometime before 1914. This line introduced new and interesting forms; many are in the Art Nouveau style and simply glazed in ivory, with sepia accents. Its simplicity may be the reason it holds little importance in collectors' eyes.

While the glaze and some of the forms may leave something to be desired, seeking out the most interesting pieces for your collection should be worth the effort.

Jardinière, Clinton Ivory, panels of flowers, unmarked, 5" x 6", **$50-$75**.

Jardinière, Clinton Ivory, rare, with squirrels, birds, and owls in trees, unmarked, 7" x 8", **$400-$600**.

Jardinière and pedestal set, Clinton Ivory, embossed with vines of roses, stamped mark, 24" overall, **$500-$600**.

Umbrella stand, Clinton Ivory, impressed mark, 20-1/2", **$200-$400**.

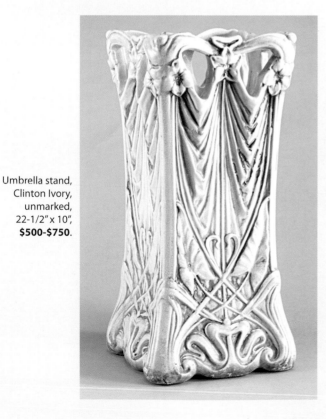

Umbrella stand, Clinton Ivory, unmarked, 22-1/2" x 10", **$500-$750**.

Blank jardinière and pedestal set, Ivory on Baldin, both pieces with impressed marks, 37", **$600-$1,000**.

CLINTON IVORY

Four Clinton Ivory pieces: an umbrella stand with classical decoration; an umbrella stand in the Baldin form; a Baldin form pedestal, 23"; and a jardinière with squirrels in the forest. Two bear impressed marks, **$300-$400**, **$200-$300**, **$200-$400**, and **$200-$400**.

Vase, Clinton Ivory, cylindrical, with rows of oak leaves, unmarked, 9-1/4" x 4-1/2", **$75-$150**.

Vase, Clinton Ivory, ovoid, embossed with squirrels and leafy branches, unmarked, 11-1/2" x 5", **$450-$650**.

CLOUDBURST

Cloudburst was produced in 1921. Pieces have lustered glazes in brown, amber, purple, and pink to name a few, with "crackled" pattern. The glaze variations keep buyers interested, although the line is not high in value much like the other luster lines of this period.

Two Cloudburst pieces: an orange bud vase and a pink faceted vase, unmarked, 6" and 8", **$50-$75** and **$100-$150**.

Bud vase, Cloudburst, corseted, red, unmarked, 6", **$100-$150**.

Bud vase, Cloudburst, trumpet-shaped, Weller Ware sticker, 9", **$250-$400**.

Vase, Cloudburst, ovoid, in brown, orange, and ivory, unmarked, 10-1/2" x 4", **$300-$400**.

COPPERTONE

Introduced in the late 1920s, most of the Coppertone pieces are relating to frogs or turtles, a few without any decoration other than its heavily mottled green glaze created to mimic the green patina found on copper. It is one of the most well-known lines Weller produced, and easily identifiable because of its bright glaze. Coppertone has been consistently popular with collectors, and while the values have dropped in recent years, the interest in it is still strong. From the common lily pad-shaped bowls and flower frogs, to the highly sought after fish-handled pitcher, Coppertone has proven time and time again to be a sound addition to any collection.

Bowl, Coppertone, perched frog and lily pads, and flower frog, marked in script, 2-1/4" x 11", **$350-$550**.

Bowl, Coppertone, flaring, paper labels and incised mark, 3" x 13-1/2" diameter **$300-$400**.

Bowl with large lily pad flower frog, Coppertone, stamped mark and paper label, 4" x 15-1/2", flower frog, 2-1/2" x 5", **$500-$700**.

Bowl and flower frog set, Coppertone, the bowl has a frog perched along the rim, stamped mark, 4" x 15-1/2", **$500-$700**.

Bowl, Coppertone, has two squared, ribbed handles on the flat rim, incised mark, 5" x 7-1/2", **$250-$350**.

Bowl, Coppertone, frog perched on the side, stamped mark, 5" x 10", **$500-$800**.

Bowl, Coppertone, flaring, incised mark, 5" x 10-1/4", **$200-$300**.

COPPERTONE

Dish, Coppertone, frog perched along the edge, incised mark, 3" x 6-1/4", **$250-$350**.

Frog fountain, Coppertone, stamped mark, 8-1/2" x 10", **$1,500-$2,500**.

Figure, frog, Coppertone, stamped mark, 2-1/4" x 2-1/2", **$150-$250**.

Figure, turtle, Coppertone, unmarked, 2-1/2" x 6", **$300-$500**.

Figure, frog, Coppertone, 3-3/4", **$200-$300**.

Figure, frog, Coppertone, unmarked, 6" x 7-1/4", **$500-$750**.

COPPERTONE

Figure, "Banjo Frog," Coppertone, 9", **$4,000-$5,000**.

Figure, dancing frogs, Coppertone, extremely rare, 16-1/2", **$7,000-$9,000**.

Vase,
Coppertone,
beaker-shaped,
etched mark,
6" x 5",
$200-$300.

Pitcher, Coppertone, bulbous, fish handle, stamped mark, 8" x 8",
$2,000-$3,000.

Pair of vases, Coppertone, bulbous,
curved handles, one incised Weller
Handmade, 6-3/4" each, **$150-$250 each**.

COPPERTONE

Vase, Coppertone, spherical, incised "E," 7" x 8-1/2", **$300-$400**.

Vase, Coppertone, bulbous with a frog perched on the rim, unmarked, 7-1/2" x 7", **$1,250-$1,750**.

Vase, Coppertone, bulbous, two frogs perched on the side, the body embossed with leaves, stamped mark, 7-3/4" x 8-1/2", **$1,000-$1,500**.

Pillow vase, Coppertone, flaring, two frogs perched on the squat base, stamped mark, 8-1/4" x 9-1/4", **$1,000-$1,500**.

Double vase, Coppertone, formed by two jumping fish, impressed mark, 8-1/2", **$1,750-$2,750**.

Pair of vases, Coppertone, flaring, with frogs clinging to the side, stamped marks, 9" each, **$400-$600 each**.

Vase, Coppertone, flaring, frog clinging to the base, covered in a dark brown to bright green glaze (possibly dark from overfiring), stamped mark, 9" x 3-1/2", **$350-$550**.

COPPERTONE

Vase, Coppertone, tall, flaring, with four frog heads around the foot, stamped mark, 11-1/4" x 5-1/2", **$1,500-$2,500.** This is a particularly nice example of this form.

Vase, Coppertone, curved handles, marked in script, 10-3/4", **$300-$500.**

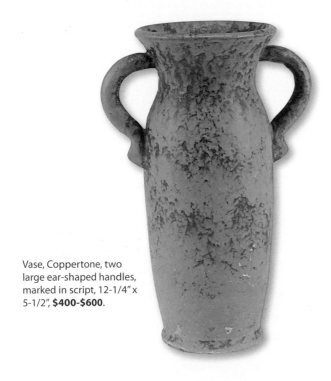

Vase, Coppertone, two large ear-shaped handles, marked in script, 12-1/4" x 5-1/2", **$400-$600.**

Vase, Coppertone, tall corseted, marked Weller Handmade in script, 12-1/4", **$500-$750.**

Vase, Coppertone, tall flaring, incised mark, 13-1/2", **$500-$700**.

Vase, Coppertone, flared, marked Weller Hand-made, 13-1/2" x 6", **$400-$600**.

Floor vase, Coppertone, flaring, unmarked, 19", **$1,500-$2,000**.

Four Coppertone pieces: a pair of lily pad-shaped vessels with a frog clinging to the side, a 4" frog figure, and a 9" bud vase with frog clinging near the base, stamped and impressed marks, **$400-$65/pair**, **$200-$300**, and **$200-$300**.

COPRA

The line collectors have coined "Copra" was produced in 1915. The background is streaked in shades of brown and painted with various flowers. The hand-painted decoration is minimal, but it does make it more valuable than the molded lines of the period. Many of the flowers are painted in the brilliant Timberlake style, though they are almost never signed by an artist.

Vase, Copra, flaring, painted with berries, blossoms, and leaves, impressed mark, 8" x 5-1/2", **$200-$300**.

Basket, Copra, painted with daisies, impressed mark, 10" x 7-1/2", **$250-$350**.

Vase, Copra, flaring, ring handles, painted with ivory and pink poppies, impressed mark, 10" x 7", **$350-$450**.

Two vases, Copra, flaring, ring handles, one painted with pansies, the other with daisies, one marked, 10" and 9", **$250-$350** and **$200-$300**.

CORNISH

CREAMWARE

Cornish was produced in 1933. The background is slightly mottled in deep blue, reddish-brown, or shaded amber. With such a limited production period, it is not as rare as you would imagine. The blue background is the most popular, and the sales of this color remain stronger than the others.

Several different variations of a Creamware line were produced in 1915. Many of the ivory-glazed pieces are decorated in the Art Nouveau style, with one variation having a Nouveau woman in profile.

Another variation of this line is called "Ethel," often with small medallions of a bun-wearing woman in profile holding a pink flower, and the cream ground is decorated with flowers and trellis-like bands at the top and bottom.

Vase, Cornish, blue, corseted, marked in script, 7-1/4" x 4-1/4", **$100-$200**.

Tobacco jar, Creamware, lidded, embossed with pipes and flowers, unmarked, 7-1/2" x 5-1/2", **$250-$350**.

Vessel, Ethel Creamware, flaring with ring handles, overflowing baskets of flowers, and maidens, unmarked, 11", **$200-$300**.

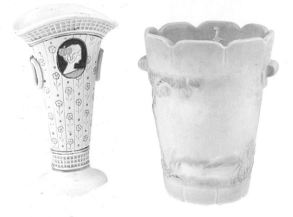

Ethel Creamware 9" flaring vase, and an 8" Senic vase, one bears stamped mark, 9" x 8", **$100-$150 each**.

CRETONE

Produced in 1934, Cretone is one of the more interesting 1930s lines, and certainly one of the most scarce. It is most often found with backgrounds in white, yellow, or black, although other colors do appear every so often. The gazelle, flower, and leaf designs are painted on in white, brown, or black over the colored glaze. This is one of Weller's most valuable lines of this period, with other 1930s lines offering little in the way of hand-painted details.

Vase, Cretone, bulbous, black decoration on an ivory ground, marked in script, artist's initials MT, 6-3/4" x 7", **$600-$800**.

Vase, Cretone, black, bulbous, with flowers and animals in ivory, signed Hester Pillsbury and incised mark, 7", **$700-$900.**

Vase, Cretone, yellow matte glaze, decoration in brown, marked in script, 8-1/4", **$600-$900**.

DUPONT

ELBERTA

Dupont was produced in the late teens. The pieces are sometimes confused with Roma, but the cross-hatched panels and topiary design sets it apart. The values are similar to those of Weller's Creamware and Ivory lines, with the exception of the large jardinières, pedestals, and umbrella stands, which bring substantially more than Ivory pieces of the same size.

The Elberta line was produced in the early 1930s. Some of the forms are molded with a snake-like or pinched design curving around the body, while others have a cupped or pinched rim, or curvy handles. They can be found in different shades of orange to green, with some examples found almost entirely in one color or the other. The forms are unusual and vary greatly, but the prices have remained very low compared to similar Weller lines of this period.

Bowl, Dupont, decorated with birds on a wire between puffy green trees, unmarked, 3-3/4" x 8", **$75-$150**.

Vase, Elberta, large bulbous, marked in script, 10" x 10", **$400-$600**.

FAIRFIELD

Produced in 1915, Fairfield pieces have bands of cherubs. It is sometimes confused with Roseville's Donatello line, but can be distinguished by the dark green and yellow or ivory glaze. Fairfield is far more rare than Donatello, but the values are only a bit higher.

Wall pocket, Fairfield, impressed mark, 9" x 5", **$100-$200**.

FLEMISH

Flemish was also designed by Rudolph Lorber. It was introduced in the mid-teens and ended in 1928, along with his Forest line. It offered many decorative styles, with each piece being a little different from the next, all in woodland themes and tones which were popular during this period.

Fish bowl holder, Flemish, shows fishing boy, 12", **$750-$1,000**.

Jardinière, Flemish, decorated with colorful birds, leaves, and flowers, unmarked, 10-1/2" x 15", **$500-$700**.

Jardinière and pedestal, Flemish, stylized four-petaled red and green flowers on an ivory ground, 36" overall, **$750-$1,250**.

Jardinière and pedestal set, Flemish, with birds and flowers on an ivory ground, unmarked, 30" overall, **$1,000-$2,000**.

FLEMISH

Planter, Flemish, covered in oak leaves, 9-1/2" x 10-1/2", **$400-$600**.

Planter, Flemish, footed, band of leaves and fruit, unmarked, 10-1/2" x 12", **$250-$350**.

Umbrella stand, Flemish, decorated with maidens, chains of pink flowers, and ivy, impressed mark, 20", **$750-$1,250**.

Umbrella stand, Flemish, unmarked, 20-1/2" x 10-3/4", **$500-$700**.

Umbrella stand, Flemish, unmarked, 22" x 10-1/2", **$450-$650**.

Vase, Flemish, corseted, rare form, decorated with branches, and small medallions with perched yellow birds, impressed mark, 7-1/2" x 6", **$600-$800**.

Vase, Flemish, cylindrical, has a red rose "tied-on" by a blue ribbon, impressed mark, 8-3/4" x 2-1/2", **$100-$200**.

FLORALA

Produced from 1915 to 1920, Florala pieces are glazed primarily in ivory or green, with colorful bands or clusters of small blossoms. Several wall pockets were produced with this line, all of which are collectible, but are not very high in value.

Wall pocket, Florala, conical, unmarked, 9-1/2" x 5", **$250-$350**.

FOREST

The successful Forest line was designed by Lorber and introduced in the mid-teens, with production through 1928. Each piece is decorated with a wooded path, or a creek running through the forest. The forms were generally utilitarian, many being tea pots, planters or jardinière and pedestal sets. Most pieces were covered in matt glaze, but some can be found in high-gloss. While the glossy pieces are harder to find, they are only slightly more valuable. The line has been a consistent hit with buyers in recent years, appealing to a great variety of collectors. With no hand-painted artwork, much of Forest's value lies in the strength of its mold and color.

Hanging basket, Forest, unmarked, 7-3/4", **$400-$600**.

Jardinière and pedestal set, Forest, impressed mark to both pieces, 28" overall, **$1,000-$1,500**.

Pair of vases, Forest, slightly corseted, impressed marks, 8" each, **$200-$300 each**.

Two Forest high-glaze pieces: a teapot and a pitcher, both covered in glossy glaze, both marked, 6" and 5", **$250-$350** and **$200-$300**.

Umbrella stand, Forest, 22", **$1,000-$1,500**.

Two Forest pieces: a basket and a flaring vase, one marked, 9" and 8-1/4", **$300-$400** and **$200-$300**.

Vase, Forest, slightly corseted, this example has crisp decoration, impressed mark, 8" x 4", **$150-$250**.

Two flaring vases, Forest, 8" and 12", one with impressed mark, **$150-$250** and **$200-$300**.

Vase, Forest, flaring, unmarked, 7-3/4" x 5-1/2", **$200-$300**.

FROSTED MATT

Frosted Matt was introduced in 1915 and although it is of interest to collectors, a good number of the pieces seem to be undervalued. While it is wise to buy large forms when seeking a higher return on your investment, it is the smaller pieces in this line that hold greater potential for increase. The bigger pieces, particularly those with bright, complex glazes, already have strong competitive interest. The smaller pieces are often overlooked, although the glazes are just as unusual and variegated as those that sell for a great amount of money.

Vase, Frosted Matt, baluster, with heavily curdled pale lime green over sheer brown glaze, 13-1/2", **$1,500-$2,500**.

Low bowl and flower frog, Frosted Matt, covered in feathered green glaze, unmarked, 2" x 8-1/4", **$150-$250**.

Lamp base, Frosted Matt, in curdled deep blue glaze, has factory drill hole, unmarked, 9" x 4-1/2", **$450-$750**.

Vase, Frosted Matt, baluster, in feathered green and gold glaze, unmarked, 12" x 6", **$500-$700**.

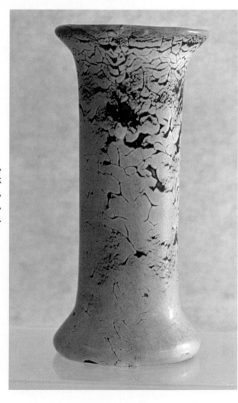

Vase, Frosted Matt, corseted, thick green curdled glaze, unmarked, **$300-$500**.

Vase, Fruitone, squat, two-handled, impressed WELLER, 5-1/4", **$350-$500**.

Fruitone was produced prior to 1920. It is covered in shaded amber, orange, and brown glaze, with black vertical streaked lines, giving it a textured look. Collectors seek the very large and rare forms produced with this line, and the prices are nearly as high as some of Weller's hand-decorated art ware. Even the smaller forms hold values as high as many art ware lines, making it one of the most sought-after commercial ware lines in recent years.

Vase, Fruitone, large squat, unmarked, 5-1/2" x 7-1/4", **$650-$950**.

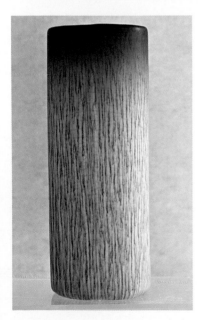

Vase, Fruitone, cylindrical, impressed WELLER, 8-3/4", **$600-$900**.

A close-up of Fruitone's streaked glaze.

GARDEN ORNAMENTS

Garden ornaments are very difficult to find because they were placed outside and broken by lawn mowers and winter weather. They are among the most valuable of all Weller Pottery, including some of the largest and rarest forms. You will find everything from colorful gnomes, to cats and birds, or cocker spaniels and terriers.

Garden ornament, Pop-Eye dog, large, marked in script, 10-1/2" x 8-1/2", **$3,000-$4,000**.

Garden ornament, figure, pelican, large and very rare, unmarked, 20" x 17", **$4,000-$6,000**.

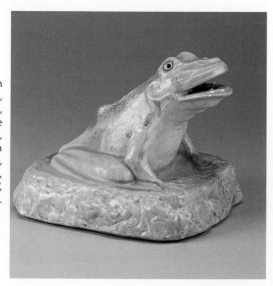

Garden ornament, fountain frog, covered in a fine yellow, brown, and pale green mottled glaze, unmarked, 10" x 11", **$1,500-$2,500**.

GARDEN ORNAMENTS

Garden ornament, figure of hen with chicks, colorful, incised mark, 8", **$2,000-$3,000**.

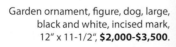

Garden ornament, figure, dog, large, black and white, incised mark, 12" x 11-1/2", **$2,000-$3,500**.

GEODE AND STELLAR

Geode and Stellar were produced in 1934. They are very similar in design, though Geode is painted with shooting stars whereas Stellar only has regular stars of different sizes and colors. Although they were both made at a time when commercial ware ruled the production lines, both lines incorporated hand-painted decoration, often with artist signatures. The backgrounds are generally pale in color, with white star designs over the top. Both Geode and Stellar are collectors' favorites, though most forms measure less than 5 inches tall and have values under $100.

Vase, Stellar, squat, ivory with blue stars, rare raised marking, 5-3/8",
$650-$850.

Vase, Geode, bulbous, white stars on a blue ground, 5-1/2",
$650-$950.

Vase, Stellar, bulbous, blue, painted by Hester Pillsbury, incised mark and artist's initials, 6" x 6-1/2", **$700-$900**.

Vase, Geode, ivory, bulbous, painted shooting star design in blue, incised mark, 3-3/4" x 4-1/2", **$500-$700**.

Vase, Stellar, ivory with blue stars, marked in script, 6-1/4",
$600-$800.

Glendale was produced throughout the 1920s; each piece has a textured background and is decorated with various birds, with some in a nest and others along the riverside. The quality and crispness of the design is of great importance when buying Glendale pieces, and can make all the difference in their value. Some can be found with such weak mold and glazing, it is hard to make out the design. Others are well colored, and sharply detailed, for which buyers will pay top dollar.

Bowl, Glendale, large, flaring, embossed with birds and waves crashing over rocks, stamped mark, 3" x 15", **$400-$600**.

Two vases, Glendale, one ovoid with a bird on a riverbank, the other bulbous with a bird amongst cattails, unmarked, 6" and 5", **$350-$500 each**.

Double bud vase, Glendale, embossed with a bluebird, nest, and berries, unmarked, 6-1/2", **$300-$400**.

Console set, Glendale, consisting of a flaring bowl, a flower frog, and a pair of candlesticks, all marked, bowl is 15" diameter, **$400-$700**.

GLENDALE

Pair of vases, Glendale, bulbous, embossed with birds standing over their nests, unmarked, 6-1/2" x 4-1/4", **$350-$550 each**.

Pair of vases, Glendale, bulbous, embossed with birds standing over their nests, unmarked, 6-1/2" x 4-1/4", **$350-$500 each**. These are the same form as shown above, but with a weaker mold and lighter glazing.

Two Glendale pieces: a wall hanging double bud vase with pocket in the center, and a gate-shaped double bud vase, unmarked, 6-3/4" and 4-3/4", **$300-$500 each**.

Vase, Glendale, bulbous, covered in pink and green matt glaze, unmarked, 7" x 5", **$250-$350**.

Vase, Glendale, bulbous, decorated with a bird in flight, stamped mark, 7" x 4-1/4", **$400-$600**.

Vase, Glendale, ovoid, embossed with birds in their nest, unmarked, 8-1/4" x 4", **$650-$950**.

GLENDALE

Vase, Glendale, ovoid, embossed with three yellow birds on a branch, unmarked, 9" x 4", **$600-$900**.

Vase, Glendale, embossed with two colorful birds on a branch, unmarked, 9" x 5", **$750-$1,000**.

Vase, Glendale, embossed by Sarah Reid McLaughlin with a bird and a nest in a tree, very crisply decorated with bright colors, embossed artist's signature, 10-1/4" x 4-1/4", **$1,000-$1,500**.

Vase, Glendale, bulbous, embossed with birds and their nest, stamped mark, 9-1/4" x 8-1/2", **$1,000-$1,500**.

Vase, Glendale, ovoid, embossed with a bird and cattails, stamped mark, 13" x 6-1/4", **$1,000-$1,500**.

Wall pocket, Glendale, cornucopia shaped, stamped mark, 12" x 6", **$450-$650**.

Vase, Glendale, baluster, embossed with birds, flowers, and butterflies, 12", **$850-$1,250**.

GRAYSTONE GARDEN WARE

Graystone Garden Ware began production in the mid to late 1920s and continued through 1941. This line consisted of mostly unglazed jardinière and pedestal sets, planters, and bird baths. The pieces were used primarily in yards and gardens, so most examples broke over the years, making it very difficult to find. Its rarity is reflected in the high prices it fetches, especially when you compare its prices to similar unglazed garden ware of the period.

Vase, Graystone Garden Ware, large, two handles, embossed with a wreath of laurel leaves, stamp mark, 15-1/2" x 13", **$400-$600**.

GREORA

Introduced in the early 1930s, Greora is similar in style and glaze to the Coppertone line. Both lines are covered in a thick mottled green glaze, but the color brown is much more prevalent on Greora. This line doesn't bring quite as much as the Coppertone line, but the prices have steadily risen in recent years.

Covered jar, Greora, marked in script, 6-1/4" x 5", **$450-$650**.

Bowl, Greora, flaring, etched mark, 2-1/2" x 14-1/2", **$200-$300**.

Vase, Greora, corseted with wide rim, unmarked, 6-1/2" x 5-1/4", **$150-$250**.

Vase, Greora, divided fan, marked in script, 7" x 7", **$250-$350**.

Vase, Greora, flaring, incised mark & Greora Ware label, 8-1/2" x 5-3/4", **$300-$500**.

Vase, Greora, bulbous with stepped body, the embossed floral band very crisp, unmarked, 9", **$250-$400**.

Vase, Greora, goblet-shaped, 9", **$300-$500**.

GREORA

Vase, Greora, bulbous, two-handles, marked in script, 10" x 6-1/2", **$400-600**.

Vase, Greora, flaring, marked in script, 11-1/2" x 6-1/4", **$400-600**.

Vase, Greora, flaring, incised mark, 11-1/2" x 7", **$300-$450**.

Wall pocket, Greora, marked in script, 10-1/2", **$250-$350.**

Vase, Greora, flaring, in unusual light brown and bright green spotted glaze, 11-1/2", **$300-$400**.

HOBART

Hobart was produced from the early through late 1920s. It includes many figural pieces, some nudes, most commonly found covered in a matt turquoise glaze. The Deco-style standing figures and their flower frogs are of particular interest to even the most advanced collector.

Figure of a woman holding her dress out to her sides, Hobart, impressed mark, 11" x 8", **$750-$1,250.**

Flower frog, Hobart, with child and duck, impressed mark, 5" x 4-1/2", **$100-$200.**

Center bowl and flower frog, Hobart, shows a young boy with a swan, marked in script, 9-1/4" diameter, **$300-$400.**

HUDSON

Produced from the early 1920s up until the mid-1930s, Hudson could possibly be the most common, and still the most collectible, of all Weller lines. The forms were used repeatedly, and even the artist would duplicate nearly exact work time and time again. Much of the painting is nice, but not outstanding. To assemble a strong collection of Hudson, seek out pieces with extensive, artist-signed decoration.

The most important pieces, known as Scenic Hudson, can be found with exceptional seascapes and landscapes, sometimes with houses, animals, or mountains.

Vase, "Hudson on Silvertone," rare and hand-carved, decorated by Dorothy England with a pelican flying beneath branches of cherry blossoms, signed D.E., 12", **$12,000-$16,000**.

Vase, Scenic Hudson, rare, painted by Hester Pillsbury with a cabin in the woods against a mountainous landscape, stamped mark and artist's signature, 9" x 4-1/2", **$2,500-$3500**.

The prices for the Hudson line greatly vary, more so than any other line. The ordinary pieces start just around $200, the large and impressive pieces, $5,000 and up. Familiarizing yourself with the forms and range of painted details will help you to easily decipher which pieces are more desirable.

Vase, Hudson, bulbous, angular handles, painted with berries and leaves, stamped mark, 6" x 5-1/2", **$350-$500.**

Vase, Hudson, two-handled, finely painted by Mae Timberlake with pink wild roses, stamped mark and artist's signature, 5-1/2" x 8", **$750-$1,000.**

Vase, Hudson, bulbous, two angular handles with pink flowers, stamped mark and illegible artist's signature, 6" x 5-1/2", **$400-$600.**

Vase, Hudson, gourd shaped, painted by Sarah Reid McLaughlin with pink and white dogwood, etched mark and artist's signature, 6-1/2", **$350-$500.**

HUDSON

Vase, Hudson, bulbous, two-handled, painted by Mae Timberlake with blue flowers on a shaded pink ground, stamped and impressed marks, artist's signature, 6-1/2" x 5-1/2", **$400-$650**.

Vase, Hudson, bulbous, two angular handles, painted by Sarah Timberlake with blue flowers around the rim, stamped mark, 6-1/2" x 5-1/2", **$400-$600**.

Vase, Hudson, extremely unusual and painted by Hester Pillsbury in shades of gray with a California pine tree in stormy landscape, incised mark and artist's signature, 7", **$2,000-$3,000**.

Vase, Hudson, bulbous, painted by Timberlake with a band of white blossoms and leaves, stamped mark and artist's signature, 6-3/4" x 6-1/2", **$400-$600**.

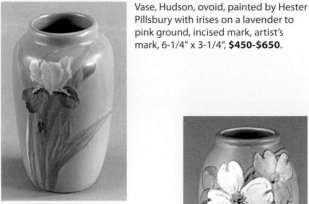

Vase, Hudson, ovoid, painted by Hester Pillsbury with irises on a lavender to pink ground, incised mark, artist's mark, 6-1/4" x 3-1/4", **$450-$650**.

Vase, Hudson, ovoid body and flaring rim, painted by Sarah Timberlake with berries and leaves, impressed and stamped marks, artist's mark, 7" x 3", **$300-$400**.

Vase, Hudson, ovoid, painted by McLaughlin with blue and white berries and leaves, impressed mark and artist's signature, 7" x 3", **$300-$500**.

Vase, Hudson, ovoid, painted with blue and white dogwood blossoms, stamped mark, 6-3/4", **$300-$400**.

Vase, Hudson, pear-shaped, painted with pink and white roses, impressed mark, 7" x 4-1/4", **$250-$350**.

Vase, Hudson, ovoid, painted by Sarah Reid McLaughlin with pink and white dogwood, stamped mark and artist's signature, 7" x 3-1/4", **$400-$500**.

HUDSON

Vase, Hudson, ovoid, painted by Hester Pillsbury with blue, pink, and yellow blossoms, stamped mark and artist's mark, 7-3/4" x 3-1/4", **$500-$750**.

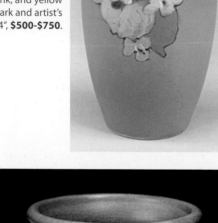

Vase, Hudson, painted by Hood with small flowers, impressed mark and artist's signature, 8", **$400-$600**.

Vase, Hudson, bulbous, two large handles, beautifully painted by Mae Timberlake with ivory and yellow roses, artist's mark only, 8" x 8", **$750-$1,000**.

Vase, Hudson, baluster, painted by Dorothy England with blue Freesia, stamped mark, 8-1/4" x 3-1/2", **$400-$600**.

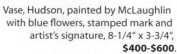

Vase, Hudson, painted by McLaughlin with blue flowers, stamped mark and artist's signature, 8-1/4" x 3-3/4", **$400-$600**.

Vase, Hudson, cylindrical, finely painted by Mae Timberlake with an iris, impressed mark and artist's signature, 9" x 3-1/4", **$600-$900**.

Vase, Hudson, bulbous, painted by Hester Pillsbury with wild roses, two of the leaves unpainted, stamped and artist's marks, 9" x 4-1/2", **$600-$800**.

Vase, Hudson, fine and large, painted by Pillsbury with yellow and blue irises on both sides, stamped mark and artist's signature, 15-1/2" x 7", **$1,500-$2,000**.

Vase, Hudson, ovoid, painted by Sarah Timberlake with lily-of-the-valley, 9", **$600-$800**.

HUDSON

Vase, Hudson, ovoid, painted by Davis with white and pink dogwood, stamped mark and artist's signature, 9" x 4-3/4", **$500-$700**.

Vase, Hudson, ovoid, painted with Hester Pillsbury with violets, impressed mark, 10" x 4", **$500-$700**.

Vase, cylindrical, believed to be an example of a rare red Hudson, incised mark, 10" x 4-1/2", **$1,500-$2,000**.

Vase, Hudson, large, finely painted by Mae Timberlake with white, pink, and blue poppies, stamp mark and artist's signature, 9-1/2" x 9-1/2", **$1,000-$1,500**.

Vase, Hudson, has two angular handles, painted by Sarah Timberlake with blue columbine on both sides, stamped and artist's marks, 10" x 5-1/2", **$600-$900**.

Vase, Hudson, fine and bulbous, painted by McLaughlin with blue columbine on a shaded blue to pink ground, impressed and artist's marks, 12" x 6", **$1,000-$1,500**.

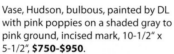

Vase, Hudson, bulbous, painted by DL with pink poppies on a shaded gray to pink ground, incised mark, 10-1/2" x 5-1/2", **$750-$950**.

Vase, Hudson, finely painted by Hester Pillsbury with branches of pink hydrangea, impressed mark and artist's signature, 12-1/4" x 5", **$1,250-$1,500**.

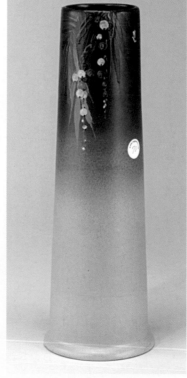

Vase, Hudson, tall tapering, painted by I.F. with berries and leaves, impressed mark and artist's initials, 12-1/2" x 3-3/4", **$450-$650**.

HUDSON

Vase, Hudson, painted by Dorothy England with blue delphiniums, stamped mark, impressed mark and artist's signature, 12-1/2" x 6", **$850-$1,350**.

Vase, Hudson, exceptional ovoid, finely painted by Ed Abel with an owl in a tree under a full moon, factory drill hole on bottom, signed E.A., 14-1/2" x 7-1/2", **$4,000-$6,000**.

Vase, Hudson Gray, tall ovoid with collared rim, finely painted by Mae Timberlake with ivory thistle on a shaded olive ground, impressed mark and artist's signature, 13-1/2" x 4-3/4", **$1,500-$2,000**.

Vase, Hudson, large, finely painted by Claude Leffler with irises on both sides, impressed mark and artist's mark, 15" x 7", **$3,000-$4,000**.

Vase, Hudson, tall, painted by Pillsbury with irises, artist signed and marked, 15" x 7", **$2,500-$3,500**.

Vase, Hudson, large bulbous, painted by McLaughlin with blue and white irises on a blue ground, incised mark and artist's signature, 15" x 7", **$2,500-$3,500**.

Vase, Hudson, large, twisted handles, painted by McLaughlin with sprays of pink and white hydrangea, marked in script and artist's signature, 16" x 7", **$2,500-$4,500**.

Vase, Hudson, fine and large, two-handles, painted by Sarah McLaughlin with blue and white irises on both sides, artist signed, 16" x 7", **$3,000-$5,000**.

HUDSON

There are many variations of the Hudson line, including Gray-on-Gray, which is decorated only in shades of gray, white, and accented with pale green.

Another variation is Hudson Light, which has a decoration with a hazy quality and is painted in pastel tones. This line is less valuable than standard Hudson, offers less variation, and rarely has an exceptional painted design or form.

Vase, Hudson Light, bulbous, painted with water lilies, impressed mark, 8", **$300-$400**.

Vase, Gray on Gray, bulbous, painted with grapes, impressed mark, 6-3/4" x 5", **$250-$350**.

Vase, Hudson Light, cylindrical, painted with daffodils, impressed mark, 8-1/2" x 3-1/2", **$300-$400**.

Vase, Hudson Light, pear shaped, painted with pink wild roses, impressed mark, 7-1/4" x 4-1/4", **$250-$350**.

Vase, Hudson Light, bulbous, painted with wild roses, impressed mark, 8-3/4" x 3-3/4", **$350-$450**.

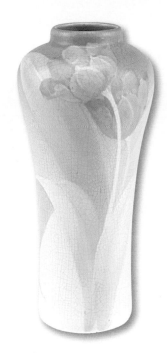

Vase, Hudson, finely painted by McLaughlin with an iris, impressed mark and artist's signature, 9-1/2" x 4", **$750-$1,000**.

Vase, Hudson Light, bulbous, painted with pink tulips, impressed mark, 10" x 4-1/2", **$400-$600**.

Vase, Hudson Light, trumpet-shaped, painted with berries and leaves, impressed mark, 10-1/2" x 5-1/2", **$400-$600**.

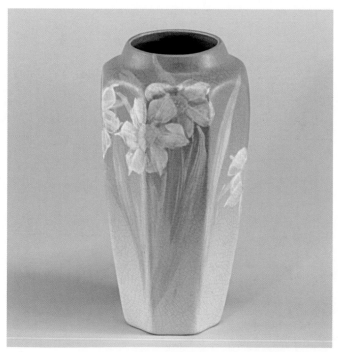

Vase, Hudson Light, faceted, painted with ivory and yellow jonquils, impressed mark, 9-3/4" x 4-3/4", **$350-$550**.

HUDSON

Vase, Hudson Light, cylindrical, painted with purple and pink berries, blossoms, and leaves, impressed mark, 11" x 4", **$400-$600**.

Vase, Hudson Light, pear-shaped, painted with yellow and white irises, stamped mark, 11-1/2" x 5-1/2", **$350-$550**.

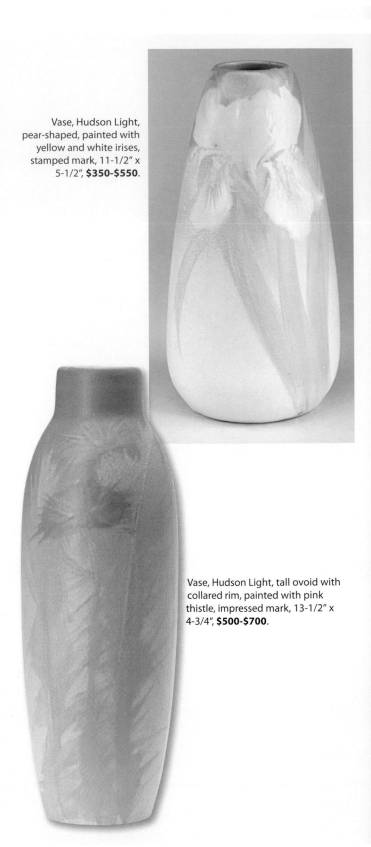

Vase, Hudson Light, faceted, painted with pink and white dogwood, impressed mark, 12" x 5-1/2", **$250-$350**.

Vase, Hudson Light, tall ovoid with collared rim, painted with pink thistle, impressed mark, 13-1/2" x 4-3/4", **$500-$700**.

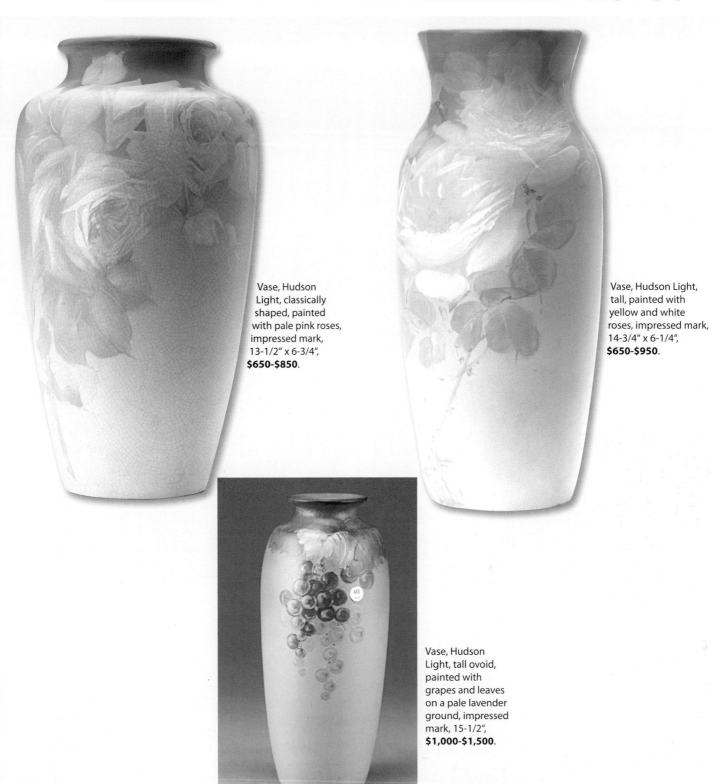

Vase, Hudson Light, classically shaped, painted with pale pink roses, impressed mark, 13-1/2" x 6-3/4", **$650-$850**.

Vase, Hudson Light, tall, painted with yellow and white roses, impressed mark, 14-3/4" x 6-1/4", **$650-$950**.

Vase, Hudson Light, tall ovoid, painted with grapes and leaves on a pale lavender ground, impressed mark, 15-1/2", **$1,000-$1,500**.

HUDSON

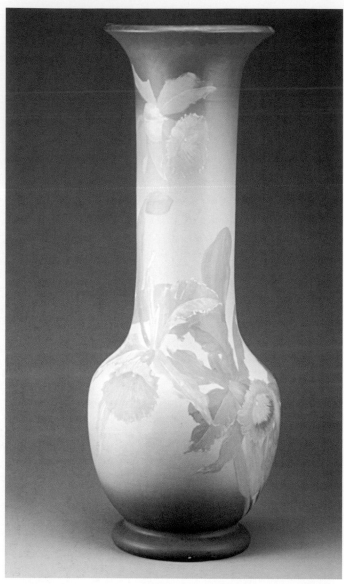

Floor vase, Hudson Light, exceptional, with tall neck, painted with orchids in green, white, yellow, and rose, impressed mark CTX-TRX, 36-1/2" x 15", **$6,000-$8,000**.

Floor vase, Hudson Light, painted with poppies, impressed mark, 22-1/2" x 9", **$2,500-$4,500**.

Hudson Perfecto was brought to market in the early 1920s. It differed from the typical slip-decorated pieces of the Hudson line, and the subtle designs look as if they were drawn with ink on paper. Its decoration can be compared to that of Rookwood's Wax Matt line, although Perfecto can be purchased for a fraction of the price. There are glossy examples as well, with the most common having brightly colored berries and leaves under a sheer glaze.

Vase, Hudson Perfecto, glossy, bulbous, painted by Ed Dedonatis with clusters of grapes and leaves in orange, red, and purple. Signed Weller in script and artist's mark, 3-3/4" x 4", **$350-$550**.

Vase, Hudson Perfecto, glossy, bright blue, colorful bands of berries and leaves on a bright white ground, 6", **$550-$750**.

Vase, Hudson Perfecto, bulbous, painted by Hester Pillsbury with apple blossoms on a white to blue ground, impressed mark and artist's initials, 6" x 5", **$400-$600**.

Vase, Hudson Perfecto, bulbous, painted by Hester Pillsbury with a branch of pink flowers, impressed mark and artist's initials, 6" x 5-1/4", **$400-$600**.

Vase, Hudson Perfecto, tall, painted by Claude Leffler with flowers, marked with artist's signature, **$600-$800**.

JUNEAU

Juneau was produced from the late 1920s until the early 1930s. The glazes set this line far apart from any other line, and most of the pieces are glazed in a deep pink, with hazy, red painted leaf-like designs around the rim. Depending on how a piece fired in the kiln, the painted designs can run and blur. At times you can even find an example marked with an artist's initials, such as those of Dorothy England.

Vase, Juneau, bright pink, impressed mark, 10", **$150-$250**.

KENOVA

Kenova was produced prior to 1920. The background color is a streaked deep olive green with hints of brown, most often decorated with flowers or lizards. Pieces from this line are not common, but only the rarest pieces such as the turtle vase, will bring a premium.

Vase, Kenova, with an applied turtle on the side, impressed mark, 5", **$650-$950**.

Vase, Kenova, two-handled, decorated with hanging branches of roses, unmarked, 10", **$800-$1,200**.

Two vases, Kenova, the piece with lizards is a particularly crisp and colorful example of the form, the other with fern fronds in yellow, impressed mark to one, 6" and 8-3/4", **$300-$400 each**.

Klyro was produced from the early to late 1920s and the design is similar to that of Woodrose. The background of each piece has a molded flower and grape design on a wood grain-like ground. The Klyro line was offered in several different color combinations, with unusual and easily breakable forms. In general they hold little value, but the rarest of forms will attract buyers' interest.

Four wall pockets: One Woodrose in pale blue, one basket-shaped Klyro, one tapered Klyro, and one Roma conical, all unmarked, 6-1/2″, 5-1/2″, 6-3/4″, 7″, **$75-$150 each**.

KNIFEWOOD AND SELMA

Knifewood was designed by Lorber and produced in the late teens. Despite being fairly common, it is one of the more popular lines of Weller. The designs vary greatly, from the small daisy bowl or butterfly vase, to the highly detailed peacock vase.

Selma is a variation of the Knifewood line, using the same forms and colors, but covered in a glossy glaze.

Knifewood and Selma are consistently popular with collectors, with prices hitting a record high in 2003. While the extensive modeling and appealing woodland decorations seemed to warrant such high selling prices, eager sellers flooded the market, and the high values couldn't be sustained. The prices have leveled out and while they remain strong among commercial ware, they are far more reasonable than they've been in years.

Vase, Knifewood, carved with butterflies and daisies, 4-1/4", **$300-$500.**

Fine planter, Knifewood, carved with bluebirds in an apple tree, unmarked, 6" x 7", **$750-$1,250.**

Vase, Knifewood, decorated with swans and trees, impressed mark, 5" x 3-1/2", **$400-$600.**

Vase, Knifewood, features squirrels, bluebirds, and hooded owls in a tree, impressed mark, 7" x 4", **$850-$1,350**.

Fine vase, Knifewood, carved with hooded owls in a tree under a crescent moon, unmarked, 8-1/2" x 4-1/4", **$850-$1,350**.

Vase, Knifewood, ovoid, with daisies and butterflies all covered in matt glaze, impressed mark, 7" x 4-1/2", **$350-$550**.

KNIFEWOOD AND SELMA

Vessel, Knifewood, carved with swans and cattails, unmarked, 3-1/4" x 5", **$300-$500**.

Planter, Selma, painted with birds in fruit trees, impressed mark, 6" x 6-1/2", **$600-$900**.

Jar, Selma, lidded, decorated with swans, impressed mark, 4-1/4", **$650-$950**.

Vase, Selma, bulbous, decorated with daisies and butterflies, impressed mark, 4-1/2" x 4-1/2", **$300-$500**.

Vase, Selma, bulbous, daisies and butterflies, impressed mark, 7-1/4" x 4-1/2", **$350-$550**.

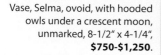

Vase, Selma, ovoid, with hooded owls under a crescent moon, unmarked, 8-1/2" x 4-1/4", **$750-$1,250**.

Vase, Selma, corseted, has colorful peacocks, flowers, and trees, impressed mark, 9" x 4-1/2", **$750-$1,250**.

Vase, Selma, carved with squirrels, owls, and bluebirds in a tree, impressed mark, 7" x 4-1/4, **$750-$1,250**.

LAMAR

Lamar was designed by John Lessell and produced from 1920 through 1925. Another of his signature luster lines, similar to his LaSa line, it features black landscapes against an almost iridescent deep ruby red ground. His luster lines are prone to scratches and glaze wear, which will greatly lessen the value if extensive.

Cabinet vase, Lamar, unmarked, 2-1/2" x 2-1/4", **$200-$300**.

Vase, Lamar, bullet-shaped, painted with pine trees on a deep red ground, marked with several paper labels, 8-1/4", **$300-$500**.

LASA

Produced from 1920-1925, LaSa was another Lessell-designed line. The ground color varies from a lustered gold, green, or red and most often features mountainous landscapes, tall trees, and a shining sun. The most rare and valuable examples are found with unusual designs such as a sailboat on the water, cabins, or a fleet of ships.

Low bowl, LaSa, painted with a landscape, unmarked, 9" diameter, **$200-$300**.

Two vases, LaSa, both with mountainous landscape and palm trees, both marked on body, 5-1/2" and 6", **$150-$250** and **$200-$400**.

Pair of bud vases, LaSa, corseted, unmarked, 7-1/4", **$200-$300 each**.

Vase, LaSa, small ovoid, finely painted with clouds and trees, unmarked, 5" x 2-3/4", **$400-$600**.

Unusual vase, LaSa, baluster, painted with green trees in front of a purple lake, green hills and a yellow sky, signed La Sa on body, 13-1/2" x 6-1/2", **$500-$700**.

Vase, LaSa, bulbous, painted with swirling clouds by Frank Dedonatis with blue berries and orange leaves, artist's mark, 4" x 4-1/2", **$300-$400**.

Vase, LaSa, large baluster, decorated with a mountains, tall trees, and a body of water, unmarked, 14" x 6-3/4", **$1,500-$2,000**.

LASA

Vase, LaSa, bullet-shaped, decorated with pine trees in front of a mountain and lake, unmarked, 6" x 3", **$250-$350**.

Vase, LaSa, pyramidal, painted with an evergreen tree and a lake landscape, marked on body, 6-1/4" x 1-3/4", **$200-$300**.

Vase, LaSa, ovoid, painted with palm trees on a golden horizon, a nicely painted example, unmarked, 6-1/2" x 3-1/2", **$300-$500**.

LOUELLA

Louella was introduced in 1915, with pale draped background and painted floral decoration. It is similar in style to Blue Drapery, but because the decoration is hand-painted and the background color differs, it is a more collectible line.

Vase, Louella, painted with irises, 9-1/2" , **$150-$250**.

John Lessell, who was known for working with metallic lustered glazes, was hired as the art director in 1920, and his first line at Weller Pottery, Lustre, was introduced soon after. Each piece is glazed in lustrous bright shades of green, blue, pink, and orange. Forms other than baskets and handled ashtrays are hard to come by, holding more value than the other more common forms. Although very basic in design, the pieces are practical and affordable, with prices starting under $25.

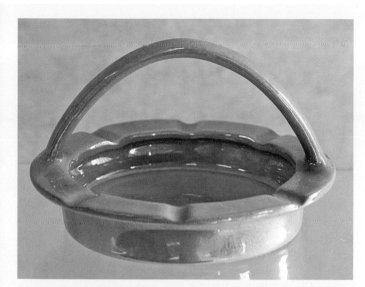

Ashtray, Lustre, handled, stamped mark, 2-3/4" x 4", **$25-$50**.

Vase, Lustre, unusual gold bulbous, Weller Ware and LP Ball Jeweler and Optometrist labels still intact, 3-3/4" x 4", **$100-$200**.

An assortment of Lustre baskets in pink, green, orange, and blue, some marked, tallest 8", **$50-$100 each**.

MALVERNE

Also spelled Malvern, this line was produced from late 1920s until 1933, and has a textured yellow or brown background and raised pink blossoms and green leaves. Though the decoration doesn't appeal to many people, the Malvern line falls into the same selling category as Tutone and Warwick, and all of this middle period commercial ware is seeing a recent surge in interest.

Two Malverne pieces: a small vase and an ovoid planter, one marked; planter, 4" x 11", **$35-$75;** vase, **$50-$100**.

Vase, Malverne, bulbous, unmarked, 5-1/2", **$75-$150**.

Pillow vase, Malverne, marked in script, 8" x 6", **$100-$200**.

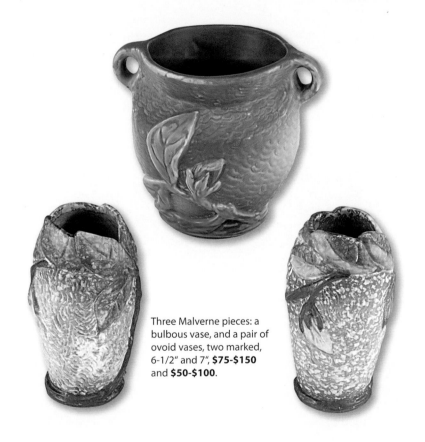

Three Malverne pieces: a bulbous vase, and a pair of ovoid vases, two marked, 6-1/2" and 7", **$75-$150** and **$50-$100**.

MAMMY

Mammy was produced in 1935 and production stopped very soon after. While it may have been considered appropriate in the 1930s, its politically incorrect design leaves a very limited group of buyers. This pattern was recently reproduced, so be sure to check for clear, crisp details on the face, with even painting to the face and arms.

MANHATTAN

Manhattan was produced from the early 1930s through 1934. The pieces are decorated with different leaf or flower patterns typically glazed in a green, but sometimes in amber or blue. The Manhattan line is somewhat scarce, though values are low to moderate for commercial wares.

Unusual vase, covered in a pink and blue mottled glaze over a Manhattan blank, unmarked, 8-1/4" x 6-1/2", **$450-$650**.

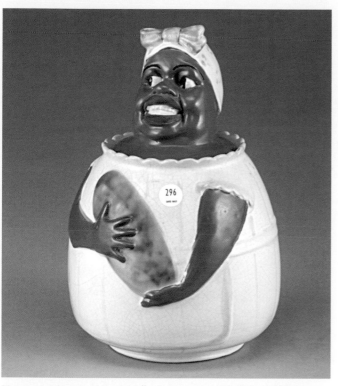

Mammy cookie jar, marked "Weller Pottery since 1872," 11-1/2" x 7", **$1,250-$1,750**.

Vase, Manhattan, green with tall leaves, marked in script, 9" x 5", **$100-$250**.

MARENGO

Created by John Lessell and produced from 1920 until 1925, Marengo is decorated with trees, most often on an orange or pink background. Marengo is quickly becoming a favorite amongst Lessel's many lustered lines, although a limited variety of forms leaves a limited market. Again, buyers are looking for glazes with little wear and crisp, clear details.

Vase, Marengo, pink, faceted, unmarked, 9-1/2" x 3-1/2", **$400-$600**.

Vase, Marengo, orange, faceted, 11-1/2", **$300-$500**.

MARVO

Marvo was introduced in the mid-1920s and production continued through 1933. The pieces are molded with tropical foliage and glazed in shades of orange or brown, pink, green, and on rare occasion they are found in blue or gray. The umbrella stands and jardinière and pedestal sets are among the more desirable molded pieces, though the small pieces are of far less interest to buyers.

Jardinière and pedestal, Marvo, brown, stamped mark, 32" overall, **$750-$1,250**.

Pitcher, Marvo, pink, unmarked, 8" x 8", **$250-$350**.

MARVO

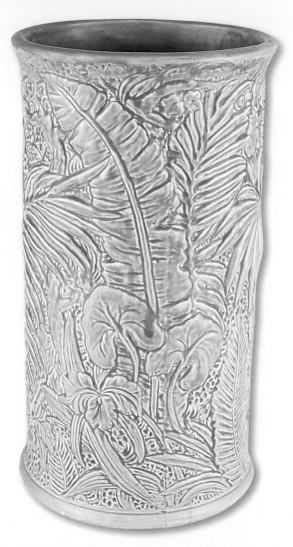

Umbrella stand, Marvo, brown, stamped mark, 20", **$750-$1,000**.

Umbrella stand, Marvo, green, ink stamp and paper label, 19-1/2" x 11", **$750-$1,000**.

Vase, Marvo, brown, bulbous, corseted, impressed mark, 8" x 5-1/4", **$150-$250**.

Jardinière, Marvo, brown, stamped marked, 10", **$150-$250**.

MINERVA

Produced in 1915, Minerva's decoration and glazes are simplistic, varying from burnt orange to a heavily curdled brown. Using only two basic colors, they created a very powerful design. It is exceedingly rare, and even the smallest and least remarkable of pieces would draw a lot of attention from buyers.

COLLECTOR TIP

Damage doesn't detract an exact amount of value from every piece. It depends on the rarity of the item, the location and extent of damage, and whether or not the piece is easily fixable, along with many other factors.

MUSKOTA

The Muskota line began production around 1915 and is made up of mostly figural pieces. The line is highly varied and quite amusing and includes everything from Victorian lady covered boxes, to large and extremely rare garden figures. The pieces are most unusual; it seemed they offered an endless variety of figures and flower frogs for sale. The frogs are decorated with swans, dragonflies, birds, women, children, fish, and crustaceans, to name just a few examples. Some are simply glazed and molded, while others are ornately decorated. The variety makes it a very collectible line and the wide range of prices makes it accessible to all buyers, and sought-after by even the most discriminating.

Figure, little girl with a watering can, Muskota or Flemish, unmarked, 6-1/2" x 4", **$500-$750**.

Figure of a woman kneeling on rocks, Muskota/Flemish, unmarked, 7", **$350-$500**.

Fish bowl holder with playful cat figure and trunk-shaped bud vase (sometimes seen fitted as a lamp), Muskota, impressed mark, 11" x 11-1/4", **$1,250-$1,750**.

Fish bowl holder, Muskota, playing cat, impressed mark, 10" x 11", **$1,750-$2,750**.

MUSKOTA

Two cats on a fence, Muskota, flower pots on each end, 7-1/4",
$750-$1,000.

Double bud vase, Muskota, two cats on a fence, unmarked, 7-1/4",
$750-$1,000.

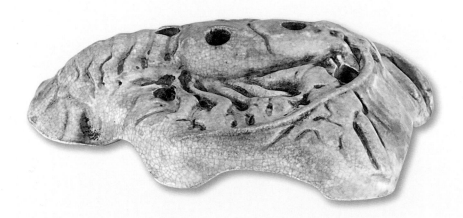

Flower frog, Muskota, lobster, impressed mark, 1-1/2" x 6", **$250-$350**.

Flower frog, Muskota, swan, unmarked, 2-1/2" x 5-1/2", **$300-$500**.

Flower frog, Muskota, with a fly on a mushroom, unmarked, 2-1/4" x 3-1/2", **$250-$400**.

Flower frog, Muskota, shaped as a frog perched on a rock, impressed mark, 3-3/4" x 5-1/4", **$400-$600**.

MUSKOTA

Flower frog, Muskota, turtle, 4" x 5", **$200-$400**.

Flower frog with two fish swimming around a log, Muskota, covered in glossy green glaze, impressed mark, 5" x 4", **$250-$400**.

Flower frog, Muskota, frog on a white water lily, impressed mark, 5" x 4-3/4", **$200-$300**.

Flower frog, Muskota, with chicks, a rare example with holes for flowers, 5-1/2" x 4-1/2", **$600-$800**.

Flower frog, Muskota, with a nude figure seated on rocks, 8", **$450-$750**.

Flower frog, Muskota, figure of a boy fishing, unmarked, 7" x 5", **$250-$350**.

Flower frog, Muskota, crab, impressed mark, 11-1/2" x 5", **$100-$200**.

MUSKOTA

Planter, turtle, Muskota, with attached water lily flower frog, 4-1/2" x 9", **$350-$500**.

Figural dish or planter, Muskota, swan, unmarked, 5", **$600-$900**.

NEISKA

NOVELTY

Neiska was produced only in 1933. The bodies are often handled, with some ornate and twisted. The exterior is glazed in mottled blue or yellow, and the interior in white semi-gloss. The value of this line is limited because of the lack of variation in designs.

Produced in the 1930s, this line consists of many small items that were suitable for gift giving, including figural soap dishes and ashtrays. It is a fun line with an unusual variety of items, but prices generally do not exceed $150.

Vase, Neiska, blue bulbous with twisted handles, incised mark, **$100-$200**.

Large and small dachshunds, Novelty, both marked, 5" x 3", **$100-$150** and **$75-$125**.

ORRIS

Orris was introduced in 1915. Each piece is covered in dark green matt glaze with brown accents, as if dark clay is showing through on the high points. Neither the wall pockets nor the vases have any great value, even those of substantial size.

Wall pocket, Orris, with flowers and trellis pattern, unmarked, 8" x 4-1/2", **$100-$200**.

Wall pocket, Orris, trellis-form, with large flowers in brown and green glaze, 8", **$100-$150**.

PARAGON

Paragon was produced in 1935. The pieces have a flower and leaf pattern, similar to Deco designs commonly seen on European pottery. It was most commonly offered in blue, orange, and deep red, with the orange being the most unusual and collectible at the moment. Paragon's prices can be high for commercial ware, dependant on the color and form.

PARIAN

Parian was produced in 1924. The pieces have diamond-shaped floral designs on a grayish matt ground. The line offered limited forms: wall pockets, hanging baskets, and simple vases, all holding little value.

Wall pocket, Parian, in pale blues and ivory on a grayish ground, unmarked, 8" x 4-1/2", **$200-$300**.

Wall pocket, Parian, in pale blues and ivory on a pale gray ground, unmarked, 10-1/2" x 6", **$300-$400**.

Hanging basket, Parian, conical, unmarked, 9-1/4" x 5-3/4", **$100-$200**.

PATRA

Patra was produced from the late 1920s until 1933. Although the length of production seems long, the pieces do not come up for sale often. Due to their rarity and the unusual forms included in the Patra line, most pieces under 5 inches sell in the $100-200 range, which is high for commercial ware of this size.

Vessel, Patra, handled, incised mark, 4-3/4" x 6", **$100-$200**.

PATRICIA

Patricia was produced in the early 1930s, and each piece is formed as a duck. All are glazed in slightly sheer pastel tones, such as apricot, green, and ivory. The vases are much more interesting and rare compared to the bowls, and the sales prices reflect this.

Form duck planter or bowl, Patricia, covered in an Evergreen glaze, incised mark, 8" x 16", **$150-$250**.

PIERRE

Pierre was produced in the mid-1930s. It was comprised of basket-weave pattern tea set pieces, the most desirable being the teapots. The pieces often have dark and extensive crazing and are likely to have chips because they were used over the years. Most pieces are valued in the $10-50 range, though some of the teapots will bring up to $100 in pristine condition.

POP-EYE DOG

A rare variation of Weller's garden ware line, this line includes figures of dogs with large eyes, and glazed in white with black or brown spots. Like Weller's garden ornaments, these are often damaged, and are difficult to find in any condition.

Pop-Eye Dog in black with unusual hazy blue eyes, marked in script, 4", **$650-$900**.

Large Pop-Eye Dog figure, covered in a brown and green feathered matte glaze, unmarked, 4-3/4" x 11", **$2,000-$3,000**.

Pop-Eye Dog in brown and black, marked in script, 4", **$600-$800**.

Pop-Eye Dog figure, marked in script, 10-1/4" x 7-1/2", **$3,000-$5,000**.

PUMILA

Pumila was introduced in the early 1920s, continuing production through 1928. The glazes vary from shaded brown and orange to green and yellow. The bright green pieces are very different in comparison to the shaded brown forms, and look as if they could be from a separate line entirely. None of the pieces are of any great value, although the brown vases and large flaring bowls are the most sought-after of all the forms.

Seven Pumila pieces: two bowls and five candlesticks, all in bright green and yellow glaze, some marked, 3" each, **$25-$50 each**.

Three bowls, Pumila, all in bright green and yellow glaze, all marked, 4" x 7-1/2", **$50-$100 each**.

Two bowls, Pumila, one large brown and one small green, 12" and 8-1/2" diameter, **$150-$250** and **$100-$200**.

PUMILA

Vase, Pumila, brown, flaring, stamped mark, 10-1/4" x 6", **$150-$250**.

Four Pumila pieces: three candlesticks, one green and two brown, and a brown water lily flower frog, 2" and 3-1/2", **$25-$50** or **$50-$75 each**.

ROCHELLE

Produced from the early 1920s through 1935, Rochelle is another variation of the Hudson line. The background colors range from deep yellow to brown, with a slip-painted floral decoration. Although it was produced for nearly 15 years, very few pieces from this line can be found. The ones that do appear for sale bring slightly more than a typical Hudson piece, which seems inexpensive considering their rarity.

Vase, Rochelle, painted by Claude Leffler with pink and yellow nasturtium, 6-1/4", **$450-$650**. This example is extremely rare because Rochelle is rarely signed by anyone other than Pillsbury.

Vase, Rochelle, bulbous, painted by Hester Pillsbury with blue and yellow flowers, a highly decorated example, incised mark and artist's initials, 6-1/2" x 3-1/4", **$700-$900**.

ROMA

Roma was designed by Rudolph Lorber and produced from 1914 until the late 1920s. The pieces have an ivory background, usually accented with garlands of flowers in pinks, greens, and reds. This line is likely to have hairlines, as are most Creamware lines. Roma does not offer many surprises, nor does it command a lot of money, but it does offer a great variety of shapes and sizes.

Bowl, Roma, footed, decorated with garlands and a medallion with bird, unmarked, 5-1/4" x 11", **$75-$150**.

Two Roma pieces: a bowl and a footed dish, one has impressed mark, 3" and 5-1/2", **$35-$75** and **$50-$100**.

Planter, Roma, large ovoid with clusters of red roses, unmarked, 5-1/2" x 16", **$300-$400**.

Jardinière and pedestal set, Roma, 30", **$500-$750**.

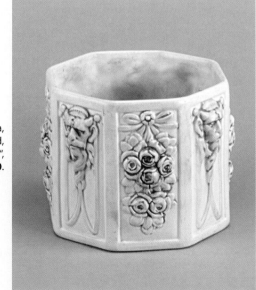

Planter, Roma, faceted, unmarked, 6-1/2" x 7", **$75-$150**.

Large planter, most likely from the Roma line, embossed with a band of fruit, flowers, and corn, unmarked, 11" x 13", **$250-$350**.

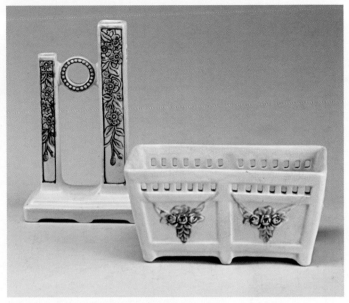

Two Roma pieces: a 6-1/2" double bud vase and a rectangular planter, one has impressed mark, **$75-$150 each**.

Two Roma pieces: a footed bowl, **$75-$150**, an a pair of triple bud vases, 7", **$50-$100 each**.

Vase, Roma, buttressed, decorated with grapes, unmarked, 10" x 4-1/2", **$150-$250**.

ROMA

Two vases, Roma, with panels of grapes and pinecones, unmarked, 10-1/4" and 7", **$75-$125** and **$50-$100**.

Wall pocket, Roma, with swags of red roses, impressed mark, 7-1/4", **$75-$150**.

Wall-pocket, Roma, decorated with large basket of pink flowers, 10-1/4", **$150-$250**.

Vase, Roma, bottle shaped, 13-1/2", **$200-$300**.

Two wall pockets, Roma, conical, one is 7-3/4" and one 8-1/4", impressed mark to one, **$75-$150 each**.

Bowl, Rosemont, low, pink Glasgow rose design, impressed mark, 9" diameter, **$50-$100**.

Rosemont was produced in the late teens to the late 1920s. A completely dissimilar line was produced in the 1930s by the same name. The early line has floral and fruit designs in glossy glaze and almost always on a black ground; on rare occasion a piece can be found with a glossy white background.

The low bowls with pink roses are the most common of all the Rosemont forms, holding very little value; the vases are the least common. The pieces with blue birds are sought after by collectors; the floral lines are of less interest.

The later Rosemont line is amber or gold in color, with a large applied flower. It is entirely unrelated to the earlier line, and holds less value.

Pair of candlesticks, Rosemont, glossy black with banded red floral design, impressed mark, 8-3/4", **$200-$400 pair**.

Planter, Rosemont, unmarked, 7-1/2" x 9-1/2", **$600-$800**.

Vase, Rosemont, classically shaped, decorated with a blue jay sitting on a branch against the standard glossy black ground, impressed mark, 10", **$500-$700**.

SABRINIAN

Introduced in the late 1920s, Sabrinian is not an easy line to come by. The sheer purple, blue, pink and brown blended glaze is reminiscent of English majolica. The pieces are formed with shells and sea creatures. It is one of Weller's more imaginative and unusual lines, but is not of great value.

Pillow vase, Sabrinian, sea horses along the sides, stamped mark, 7" x 7-1/2", **$200-$300**.

Four Sabrinian pieces: two footed bowls, a round bowl, and a two-handled vase, stamped marks, tallest: 10-1/2"; footed bowls, **$100-$200 each**; round bowl, **$150-$250;** vase, **$200-$300**.

Silvertone was produced throughout the 1920s. The background is textured in shades of gray, blue, and white, with many different varieties of floral decoration, such as calla lilies and daisies. A crisp mold and strong color will add quite a bit of value. Those pieces with weaker molds and color are of much less interest to collectors.

Jardinière, Silvertone, has clusters of hydrangea, stamped mark, 11" x 10-1/2", **$600-$900**.

Console set, Silvertone, consisting of a pair of candlesticks, a flaring bowl, and a flower frog, all marked, bowl 12-1/2" diameter, **$400-$600**.

SILVERTONE

Silvertone corseted vase with irises, 5-1/2",
$350-$450.

Vase, Silvertone, gourd-shaped, twisted handles,
decorated with yellow flowers, stamped mark,
6-1/2" x 6", **$300-$400**.

Vessel, Silvertone, squat, embossed with pink
roses, strong color, stamped mark, 6-1/2" x
6-1/4", **$450-$650**.

Two vases, Silvertone,
both decorated with
yellow flowers, one with
twisted handles, the other
with branch handles,
stamped marks, 6" x 8-1/2",
$300-$400 each.

Fan vase, Silvertone, embossed with purple thistle and applied leaves, stamped mark, 8" x 9-1/2", **$500-$700**.

Fan vase, Silvertone, unusual, embossed with dogwood blossoms, covered in matte green glaze, unmarked, 8" x 10-1/2", **$300-500**.

Vase, Silvertone, bulbous, embossed with lilies, stamped mark, 9-1/2" x 5-1/2", **$250-$350**.

Vase, Silvertone, bulbous, decorated with large pink chrysanthemums, stamped mark, 9" x 5-1/2", **$300-$500**.

Vase, Silvertone, ovoid, two-handled, embossed with dogwood, stamped mark, 9-1/4" x 6", **$300-$400**.

Vase, ovoid, Silvertone-type, decorated by Dorothy England with flowers, signed D.E., 10", **$1,250-$1,750**.

SILVERTONE

Vase, Silvertone, bottle-shaped, embossed with white lilies, stamped mark, 11-1/2" x 5-3/4", **$350-$550**.

Vase, Silvertone, corseted, with branches of pink and white dogwood, stamped mark, 10-1/2" x 6-3/4", **$350-$500**.

Vase, Silvertone, large, flaring, with white calla lilies and daisies, stamped mark, 10-3/4" x 7", **$350-$500**.

Four Silvertone pieces: a vase with poppies and butterflies, 12-1/4"; a bulbous vase, and a pair of candlesticks, all marked, **$450-$650, $300-$500, and $250-$450 a pair**.

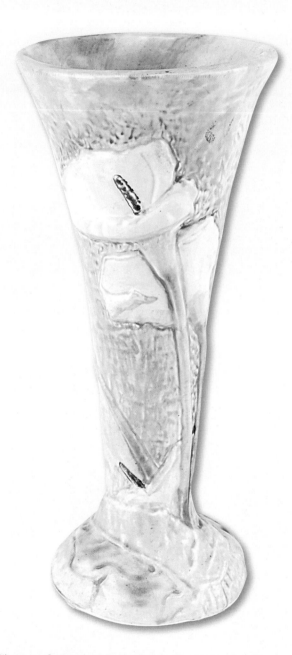

Wall pocket, Silvertone, decorated with yellow roses, strong color and mold, stamped mark, 10" x 5-1/4", **$350-$450**.

Vase, Silvertone, flaring, decorated with calla lilies, stamped mark, 11-3/4" x 5", **$350-$500**.

SOUEVO

Souevo was introduced in 1910. It imitates Native American ceramics and is comparable in value to similar lines produced by Clifton Pottery and Owens, though even the largest forms are not very valuable.

Jardinière, Souevo, has a band of snail-like designs near the rim, unmarked, 7-1/4" x 9-1/4", **$200-$400**.

Three Souevo pieces, a bowl and two vases, one stamped Weller, 4", 4-3/4", 3", **$50-$100, $75-$150,** and **$100-$150**.

Two vases, Souevo, similar form with bright black and white painted designs, unmarked, 6" and 7", **$100-$200 each**.

SOUEVO

Three vases, Souevo, one corseted and two bulbous of similar form, unmarked, 10-1/2", 5", 4-1/2", **$150-$200, $75-$150**, and **$75-$150**.

Wall pocket, Souevo, conical, unmarked, 12-1/4", **$200-$300**.

Vase, Souevo, squat, with geometric design in black and white, unmarked, 4-1/2" x 7", **$100-$200**.

Wall pocket, Souevo, on Parian blank with black bands on a brown ground, unmarked, **$100-$200**.

TIVOLI

Introduced in 1920, every Tivoli piece is covered in an off-white glossy glaze with black trim and bands of colorful flowers. It is almost identical to a Zona design, but it lacks the vertical blue ribbed design on the ivory body.

Wall pocket, Tivoli, conical, impressed mark, 9-3/4" x 5", **$75-$150.**

TURKIS

Turkis was produced from the late 1920s until 1933. It is a deep glossy red with frothy dripping mustard and olive glaze over top. It is simple in its design, but the line is fairly difficult to find, so the pricing is moderate to high for undecorated commercial ware.

Two Turkis pieces: a flaring vase and a bulbous vase with twisted handles, marked in script, 6-1/2" x 7-1/4", **$75-$125 each.**

Vase, Turkis, flaring, marked in script and Turkis paper label, 8-3/4" x 6", **$100-$200.**

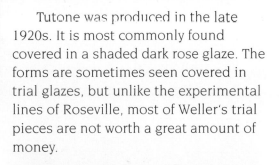

Tutone was produced in the late 1920s. It is most commonly found covered in a shaded dark rose glaze. The forms are sometimes seen covered in trial glazes, but unlike the experimental lines of Roseville, most of Weller's trial pieces are not worth a great amount of money.

Console set, Tutone, green, comprised of a three-sided bowl and a pair of candlesticks, stamped mark, bowl 3-1/2" x 7", **$250-$350/set.**

Unusual vase with blue, green, and white mottled glaze on a Tutone blank, unmarked, 6" x 6-1/2", **$100-$200.**

Vase, Tutone, three-sided, unmarked, 9" x 5-1/2", **$250-$350.**

Vase, Tutone, rare, green leaf design around the rim, 12-3/4", **$500-$800.**

VELVA

Produced from 1928 to 1933, Velva colors range from deep blue to brown, with rectangular panels of flowers and leaves. If the simple floral designs are crisply molded, and the form is atypical, such as a lidded ginger jar, the prices can exceed the "standard" for commercial wares.

Vase or ginger jar, Velva, brown, lidded, marked in script, 11-1/4" x 6", **$350-$450**.

WARWICK

Produced in the late 1920s, Warwick's heavily textured background ranges from reddish-brown to a deep chocolate, with molded branches and flowers over top. It is somewhat busy, but the forms keep collectors interested. This is the type of piece you are likely to find on a flea market table or on a shelf at a house sale. Although values on the common pieces do not exceed $150, the values of the larger and more complicated forms have risen above that mark.

Planter, Warwick, two-handled, impressed mark, 4-1/2" x 9-3/4", **$75-$150**.

VOILE

Voile was produced from the early 1920s through 1928. It is uncommon, but the line did not offer many large or important forms. The jardinière and pedestal sets draw the most attention and are priced higher than most molded sets of that period.

Potpourri jar, Warwick, lidded, 5", **$200-$250**.

Two Warwick pieces: a double bud vase and a basket, 8-1/2" and 9", **$100-$150** and **$200-$250**.

Three Warwick pieces: pillow vases, 4-1/2" and 7-1/2"; and a planter, 6", **$75-$125, $100-$150**, and **$100-$200**.

Vessel, Warwick, unusual basket shape, stamped mark, 7" x 7", **$150-$250**.

Wall pocket, Warwick, stamped mark, foil Weller label, and Weller Warwick Ware paper label, 11", **$150-$250**.

Vase, Warwick, footed, cylindrical body, unmarked, 10" x 4-1/2", **$150-$250**.

Pillow vase, Warwick, stamped mark, 10" x 7", **$100-$200**.

WILD ROSE

Wild Rose was produced from the early to mid-1930s. The background is either green or pale orange, with large branches of white roses. It is one of the more popular commercial ware floral lines, although only the largest forms bring more than $100. The small forms are collectible, but generally fetch no more than $50.

Two Wild Rose tall pieces: a bulbous vase and a ewer, in pale orange and green blended glaze, marked in script, **$75-$125 each**.

WOODCRAFT

Woodcraft was produced from 1920 through 1933 and features woodland creatures and tree-like forms in shades of brown and green, sometimes with brighter accents in reds, blues, ivory, or yellow. It is probably Weller's most extensive line, offering both very common forms worth little more than $100, and large and unusual forms bringing in excess of $1,000. Because of the vast number of designs to choose from, it has remained a collector's favorite for many years.

Bookends, Woodcraft, rare, features an owl, unmarked, 5-1/2", **$800-$1,200**.

Bowl, Woodcraft, with panels of squirrels in the forest, stamped mark, 6" diameter, **$150-$250**.

Candlestick converted into a lamp base, Woodcraft, rare, with owls perched around the rim, unmarked, 13", **$700-$900**.

Dish, Woodcraft, with a squirrel perched on the side, 5-1/2", **$200-$350**.

Figure or bookend, Woodcraft, with a pair of hunting dogs in tall grass, impressed mark, 7" x 11-1/2" x 5", **$1,500-$2,000**.

WOODCRAFT

Hanging basket, Woodcraft, large, with owls in a tree, 4-3/4" x 10", **$200-$300**.

Jardinière, Woodcraft, rare, cats chasing birds through twisted vines and flowers, 7-3/4" x 9", **$750-$1,000**.

Jardinière, Woodcraft, has a woodpecker perched on the side, 8" x 5-1/2", **$400-$600**.

Mug, Woodcraft, embossed with foxes in their den, impressed mark, 6" x 5-1/4", **$400-$600**.

Pair of vases, Woodcraft, embossed with foxes in their den, impressed marks, 6" x 7", **$250-$350 each**.

Planter, Woodcraft, with daffodils and mushrooms, impressed mark, 5-1/2" x 10", **$350-$500**.

Planter, Woodcraft, cylindrical, decorated with foxes in their den, unmarked 6" x 7", **$300-$500**.

WOODCRAFT

Planter, Woodcraft, large and rare, woodpecker perched on the side, unmarked, 8" x 11", **$600-$900**.

Tankard, Woodcraft, embossed with foxes in their den, impressed mark, 13" x 7", **$800-$1,200**.

Bud vase, Woodcraft, rare, unmarked, 7-1/4" x 6-1/4", **$400-$500**.

Bud vase, Woodcraft, impressed mark, 8-1/4" x 3", **$100-$200**.

Vases, Woodcraft, slightly corseted, decorated with branches of pink blossoms, unmarked, 10-1/4" each, **$150-$200 each**.

Double bud vase, Woodcraft, formed with two trees connected by branches of apples, unmarked, 7-1/2" x 8", **$100-$200**.

Double bud vase, Woodcraft, owl perched on the top, impressed mark, 14" x 7-1/2", **$500-$750**.

WOODCRAFT

Vase, Woodcraft, fine and large, tree-shaped with an applied owl perched on a branch, unmarked, 15-1/2" x 6-1/2", **$1,000-$1,500**.

Vase, Woodcraft, tree-shaped, impressed mark, 10-1/2" x 4-1/4", **$75-$150**.

Vase, Woodcraft, corseted, shows branches of fruit, unmarked, 12" x 6", **$350-$550**.

Two Woodcraft pieces: a bowl and a 12" flaring vase, both decorated with plums, impressed marks, **$100-$200** and **$250-$350**.

Vase, Woodcraft, tall, branch handles and an owl in a tree, impressed mark, 13-1/2" x 5-1/4", **$750-$1,250**.

Wall hanging, Woodcraft, rare, with branch-shaped pockets, decorated with large pink flowers and applied blue birds nesting in branches, impressed mark, 15" x 13", **$1,250-$1,750**.

Wall pocket, Woodcraft, red flowers on a branch, unmarked, 9", **$300-$400**.

Wall pocket, Woodcraft, decorated with an applied squirrel, a very nice example of this form, impressed mark, 9" x 4-1/2", **$350-$500**.

Two Woodcraft wall pockets: one with an owl in a tree, the other with applied squirrel, impressed mark and Woodcraft label to owl pocket, 10-1/2" and 9", **$300-$500 each**.

Wall pocket, Woodcraft, large with owl in a tree, a very crisp example, unmarked, 10-1/2" x 6", **$300-$500**.

WOODROSE

Produced before 1920, Woodrose's barrel-like forms are decorated with pink roses. It is one of the least valuable lines of this period.

Three Woodrose pieces: a bowl, a planter, and a 10" vase, all with impressed marks, **$50-$100**, **$25-$50**, and **$50-$100**.

Wall pocket, Woodrose, unmarked, 6-3/4" x 3", **$75-$120**.

XENIA

Xenia was probably introduced sometime between 1910-1914. The matte background most often varies from deep blue-green to lighter blue-gray, in Arts and Crafts floral patterns. It is a popular line, attracting buyers from all ends of the collector's spectrum.

Another line is also known as Xenia, completely dissimilar from the first. It is a Creamware-type line, with subdued hand-painted floral decoration.

Lamp base, Xenia, finely decorated with pink flowers on a matt deep green-blue ground, impressed mark, 14-1/4", **$1,500-$2,000**.

Vase, Xenia, ovoid, white circular flowers, 5-1/4", **$1,250-$1,500**.

Introduced in 1920, Zona was designed by Lorber. This high-glaze line encompasses a great variety of designs and colors. For example, they produced dinnerware with a Baldin-type apple pattern, a variety of pitchers, children's dishware, and highly detailed vases. This diversity makes it a particularly collectible line.

Table lamp, Kingfisher, rare, possibly from the Zona line, impressed mark, 13", **$1,500-$2,000**.

Flower frog, large, kingfisher, possibly Zona or Brighton, impressed mark, 9" x 7", **$200-$350**.

Pitcher, Zona, shows ducks splashing in puddles, impressed mark, 7-1/2" x 7", **$150-$250**.

Jardinière and pedestal set, Zona, columns and bands of flowers in polychrome, unmarked, 32-1/2" overall height, **$650-$950**.

ZONA

Unusual pitcher, most likely from the Zona line, embossed with yellow flowers, unmarked, 7-1/2" x 9", **$250-$350**.

Pitcher, Zona, with lightly colored panels of kingfishers and cattails, impressed mark, 8-1/2" x 9", **$200-$300**.

Plates, lunch and dinner, Zona, some with stamped mark, 7-1/2" and 9" diameter, **$30-$50 each**.

TILES AND HAND-DECORATED WARES

Weller also produced tiles during the mid to late 1930s, yet they are almost unattainable. It would be nearly impossible to price a nicely decorated Weller tile because there are few sales records on which to base its worth.

All hand-decorated wares were discontinued in 1935, at which time Weller began to produce strictly molded pottery. Weller finally closed its doors in early 1948, long after the company produced its last piece of art ware.

Two pieces: a Roma footed dish, and a Clinton Ivory jardinière on a Zona blank, both unmarked, 5-1/2" and 8-3/4"; jardinière, **$75-$125**; dish, **$50-$75**.

Jardinière and pedestal set, in matte blue with classical masks and acanthus leaves, unmarked, 32" overall, **$1,250-$1,750**.

Jardinière and pedestal set, unusual, embossed with plants and butterflies under a pink, green, and brown majolica-type glaze, unmarked, 32" overall, **$700-$900**.

Three pieces: a Burntwood bulbous vase with Glasgow roses, 7-1/2"; the other with mythological decoration (this has a very weak mold), and a Silvertone flower frog, frog bears stamped mark, **$150-$250, $75-$150**, and **$50-$100**.

Four wall pockets: One Clinton Ivory/Knifewood with daisies, one Souevo with banded black swirled design, one large Parian form in Souevo glazes, and one Golbrogreen, 5-1/2", 8-1/2", 10-1/4", and 8-1/2", **$100-$200 each**.

Four wall pockets: One double Sydonia, one Arcadia, one Oak Leaf, and one Darsie in green-blue, all marked, the Sydonia with original paper label, 9", 9", 8-1/4", 9", **$75-$150 each**.

Other pottery lines

This book has focused on Weller's most collectible, most common, and also the most unusual designs. Many of Weller's lines have been left out of this book; some are too rare to obtain an image, and others that are very common and low in value. Most of these lines are listed here, along with production dates and a description of the designs, when possible.

Alvin

Alvin was produced in 1928. It shares many forms with the Woodcraft line, but the glaze differs. Woodcraft is a medium to dark blue, while Alvin comes in a glossy, sheer, light brown.

Arcadia

Arcadia was produced from the mid to late 1930s. It is one of the few later high-glaze lines Weller produced, in shades of blue, pink, yellow, and white. The bodies have various molded leaf designs.

Arcola

Arcola was produced in 1920. It has a glossy, dark blended glaze, with applied grapes and roses.

Breton

Breton was produced in the early to late 1920s. Most pieces are glazed in one solid color, including the banded floral design, although they can be found in two-color designs as well.

Brown and White

Brown and White was produced in 1933. The kitchen pieces, including bowls, teapots, and canisters, had brown glazed exteriors and white glazed interiors. The color scheme was a perfect fit for 1970s kitchens, but hasn't really found a place in the modern home.

Cactus

Cactus was produced in the early 1930s, and if it weren't clearly marked, it would probably be mistaken for McCoy. The forms are cartoon-like, in brightly colored glossy glazes, with holes to form figural vases or dishes.

A Hester Pillsbury watercolor painting of a lady holding an umbrella, possibly done during her time at Weller, Signed H.E.P, 10-1/2" x 8", **$350-$500.**

Candis

Candis was produced in the early 1930s. The pieces were glazed in pale shades of green, yellow, and blue, with ivory floral paneled design.

Dynasty

Dynasty was produced in the late 1920s. Each piece is glazed in two shades of blue, and a pale green at the top. The vases bear ring handles, the forms similar to those used by Fulper.

Éclair

Éclair was produced in 1920. It is cream-glazed line with applied pink roses.

Florenzo

Florenzo was produced from the early 1920s until 1928. It has similarities to the Roma line. The body is always lobed with a slight flare, covered in ivory glaze with shaded green accents. Small bouquets of flowers are molded over top.

Golbogreen or Golbrogreen

This line is often seen spelled both ways; it was produced in 1903 and 1904. The bodies are heavily textured, in shaded yellow, orange, and sometimes chocolate brown or olive green.

Greenbriar

Greenbriar was produced in the early 1930s. The glaze varies from Coppertone-like green, to a dripping, foamy purple glaze. This is a rare line and while it may not be attractive to most, it is one of the higher valued lines of this period.

Lavonia

Lavonia was produced from the early 1920s until 1928, the forms covered in a shaded pale pink to purple glaze.

Lebanon

Lebanon was produced sometime after 1910. It is one of the rarest of Weller's pottery; it certainly seems the production time was limited.

Lorbeek

Lorbeek was produced from the mid-1920s until 1928. The bodies have stepped, angular sides, and are glazed in a simple off-white glaze or pastel tones.

Loru

Loru was produced from the mid to late 1930s. It came in three colors: shaded green to gold and red to brown, and shaded blue.

Four pieces: a Florenzo planter with a flower frog and lid adorned with a water lily, and three ivory floral flower frogs, one marked, planter: 7-1/2" x 6-3/4", **$75-$125**, and **$25-$50 each.**

Luxor

Luxor was produced in 1910. It is somewhat similar to Roseville's Mostique line, and while Luxor is far more scarce than Mostique, the values of both lines are nearly equal.

Marbleized

Marbleized was introduced in 1914, the multi-colored glazes marbleized just as the name suggests. It was offered in several different hues, although no one color is more collectible than another. It is unusual for being an early line, but it holds very little value or interest to the experienced collector or dealer.

Melrose

Melrose was produced in 1920. A few pieces are similar in design to the Baldin pattern, with apple design and twisted branches, others have various fruit or flowers.

Mirror Black

Mirror Black was produced before 1924. All the forms are simply glazed in glossy black.

Monochrome

Monochrome was produced from 1903-1904. The simple, utilitarian forms were glazed in muted lustered tones.

Montego

Montego was produced in the late 1920s. Every piece is covered in a distinct bright orange glaze, a foamy dark green to turquoise glaze dripping over top.

Nile

Nile was produced in the 1930s. The pieces have blended dripping glazes. Similar pieces were produced by other Ohio companies, and these are often confused with the Nile line.

Noval

Noval was produced in 1920. The glossy ivory body is trimmed with pink flowers and/or apples, and black trim.

Panella

Panella was produced from the mid to late 1930s. Each piece is shaded in blue, green, or orange, with yellow pansies. One of the more desirable late floral lines, perhaps because it is one of the few that clearly differs from the others.

Pastel

Pastel was produced from the mid to late 1930s. Most pieces have a wave-like design, the matt glazes in shades of medium blue, teal and yellow.

Pearl

Pearl came to market in the late teens; the date production ceased is unclear.

Reno

Reno was produced sometime after 1910. The utility pieces are simply decorated with a striped band. They are very similar to Roseville's Utility mixing bowls, although Weller's line is less refined and less valuable.

Roba

Roba was produced from the mid to late 1930s. The pieces textured backgrounds vary from blue or green to white, or reddish brown to beige. The curved bodies and handles distinguish this line from the other similar patterns of this period, and the flowers vary from roses to gladiolas.

Rudlor

Rudlor was produced from the early 1930s until 1936 and is easily distinguished from the other 1930s floral patterns. The body is molded with slightly angled horizontal lines, with the background in white, blue-green, or apricot. Often pieces will have beaded or angular handles. It is one of the more interesting floral patterns, with a little more potential than the similar lines of that period.

Scandia

Scandia was produced in 1915. The body is glazed in black, with beige floral or linear designs, covered in a sheer glossy glaze. It is not common, but doesn't command high prices.

A Tutone bulbous vase, 7-1/2"; a Scenic double bud vase, 6-1/2"; and a Roba flaring vase, 11", all with script or stamped mark, **$50-$100 each.**

Softone

Softone was produced from the early 1930s until 1935. As the name suggests the pieces are glazed in glossy soft tones of pink, yellow, and blue. Most pieces have a draped design, although few have a wave-like design or foot.

Wall pocket, Roba, yellow, impressed mark, 10-1/2", **$75-$125.**

Underglaze Blue Ware

Underglaze Blue Ware was produced in 1915, the pieces are glazed in glossy blue, or blue flambé glaze.

Two pieces: an orange Blossom jardinière, and a green Rudlor vase, 11" and 15-1/2", **$75-$125 each.**

Chelsea Utility Ware – 1933

Blossom

Blossom was produced in the mid to late 1930s; each piece is molded with two white flowers clustered together on a branch. The blue or green bodies are either slightly lobed, draped, or have stylized handles

Darsie

Darsie was produced in 1935. Pieces are glazed in ivory, blue, and green-blue semi-matt glazes, and each is molded with tassels.

Delsa

Delsa was produced from the mid to late 1930s. The background is textured in either solid white or blue, with small clusters of different flowers, including dogwood, pansies, roses, and daisies.

Gloria

Gloria was produced sometime after 1936. The floral decoration is nearly the same as on the other 1930s floral patterns, but the burnt orange background color is slightly different. It is also offered in the green-blue glaze that seemed almost standard in the 1930s.

Ivoris

Ivoris was produced from 1933 until 1938. Weller recycled old, familiar forms and glazed them in solid ivory glossy glaze. The ivory forms are less desirable and less expensive than the forms with their original glazes.

Lido

Lido was produced from 1935 to the late 1930s. The curved body of each is shaded in blue, pink, or yellow. Most have a scalloped rim, some with a molded leaf pattern, and all with a draped or lobed body.

Mi-Flo

Mi-Flo was produced from 1935 to 1938. The background is solid white, with bright yellow floral designs. The background design can be stepped, wavy, or untextured.

Oak Leaf

Oak Leaf was introduced sometime prior to 1936; the year production ceased is unclear. The backgrounds vary from blue, green, or brown, each with oak leaf and acorn decoration. Not unattractive in design, the large and practical forms are worth their very small price tag.

Raceme

Raceme was produced in 1934. The body is multicolored, in blue and black, with painted floral designs.

Ragenda

Ragenda was produced in 1935. Each piece has a very distinct draped pattern, and comes in a variety of colors.

Seneca

Seneca was introduced in 1933. The mottled glazes in tones from peach to green are very simple, and reminiscent of Roseville's much more expensive Earlam line.

Kitchen Gem – After 1936

Bouquet

Bouquet was produced in the late 1930s. Again, this is very much like the other late floral lines, but the blue and green backgrounds are darker. It is also offered in a pale apricot color. Most of the pieces do not feature bouquets of flowers as the name suggests, but they are molded with single daisies, daffodils, branches of dogwood; the smaller pieces with petite floral designs.

Decorated Creamware

Decorated Creamware was produced in the late 1920s, and has the look of a china-painted piece.

Dorland

Dorland, introduced in 1937, is one of Weller's latest lines. Each piece is simply glazed in green-blue, the rim scalloped, and an S-like design molded into the body. A few of the pieces are molded with interesting curved handles and bubble-like design just below.

Evergreen

Evergreen has pelican forms covered in matt blue-green glaze.

Fleron

Fleron was introduced in the late 1920s, and is very simple in decoration. The body of the piece has a slight ribbing, the exterior is in shades of green, and the interior is sometimes different in color than the exterior. This is one of the few lines of Weller that has been reproduced, and it is very difficult to differentiate between new and old.

Floral

Floral was produced in 1937. Each piece has a blue-green background with tiny floral design. With nothing to set it apart from the other commercial ware floral designs, it is one of the least desirable patterns.

Golden Glow

Golden Glow was produced from the late 1920s until 1933. Each piece is covered in a pale mottled orange glaze, and is most often decorated with green leafy branches and darker orange accents. Other

Wall pocket, four parts, the Sydonia blank covered in a mottled turquoise glaze, impressed mark, 9", **$250-$350**.

Vase, Velvetone, matt green, raised stylized designs, covered in vellum glaze, marked with Velvetone Ware paper label, 6" x 5-3/4", **$400-$600**.

styles were offered as a part of this line, some of the forms with waves, birds, or sometimes unadorned. Most forms are under 6 inches, with price tags in the $100-$175 range, which is high for late commercial ware with molded decorations.

Raydance

Raydance was produced after 1936. The bodies are molded with vertical ribbed design, raised floral and leaf patterns, and a round notched base.

Senic/Scenic

Introduced in 1937, Senic is pale green with tree-lined landscapes, from palms to pines. It is one of the few late commercial ware lines with most pieces valued in excess of $100.

Sydonia

Sydonia was produced from the late 1920s until 1933. The leaf-like bases are glazed in deep green, the upper body in mottled blue.

Velvetone

Velvetone was produced in the late 1920s. It can be found glazed in varying soft tones.

Miscellaneous

Many pieces simply cannot be classified. Weller sometimes worked with trial glazes or experimented with new forms.

Fakes have also been found, most originating from Asia, but others appear to be very early American imitations of Weller Pottery. A fake can almost always be given away by the clay. Ohio clay has a rich yellowish color, which you will not find on the later copies.

Vase, three-handled, covered in a turquoise and blue crystalline glaze, incised mark, 5" x 6-1/2", **$250-$350**.

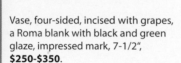

Vase, four-sided, incised with grapes, a Roma blank with black and green glaze, impressed mark, 7-1/2", **$250-$350**.

Vase, cylindrical, hand carved by Timberlake with a woodpecker on a tree, signed on body, 8", **$3,500-$5,000**. Many collectors call this unusual hand-carved style of decoration "Hudson on Silvertone."

Reverse side of the cylindrical vase on the left.

Fake Fleron bulbous vase with mottled pink interior and pale turquoise exterior, marked "Weller Handmade" in ink, 8-1/4" x 5-1/4", **$20-$40**.

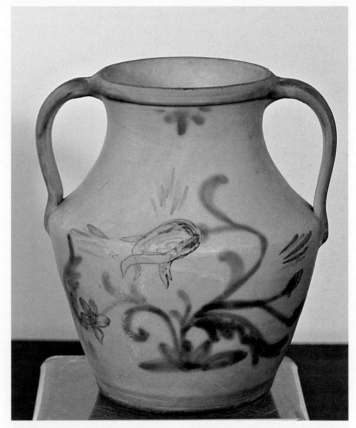

Vase, rare, crackled white, footed, with stylized floral silver appliqué, marked in script, 10" x 5", **$600-$900**.

Vase, two-handled, yellow, painted with flowers, most likely by Dorothy England, incised mark and "L," 8-1/2", **$750-$1,000**.

Vase, unusual, covered in a blue crystalline glaze, very similar to that of Roseville's Crystalis line, incised mark, 11", **$1,000-$2,000**.

Price Guide

Ashtray, Lustre, handled, stamped mark, 2-3/4" x 4". . . . . **$25-$50**

Basket, Copra, painted w/daisies, impressed mark, 10" x 7-1/2". .**$250-$350**

Batter jug, Ansonia, covered in a mottled green and yellow glaze, signed
Weller in script, 10" x 8" . . . .**$100-$200**

Biscuit jar, Turada, with an ivory foliate decoration on an indigo ground,
impressed Turada mark, #615, 6-3/4" x 5-1/2" . . . .**$250-$350**

Bookends, Woodcraft, rare, features an owl, unmarked, 5-1/2"
. . . .**$800-$1,200**

Bowl

Ardsley, flaring, stamped mark. **$265**

Ardsley, flaring, stamped mark, 4-1/2" x 8". . . . .**$250-$350**

Bonito, low, painted with swirled design and lily-of-the-valley, marked in
script, 9-1/4" dia. . . . .**$100-$200**

Coppertone, perched frogs and lily pads, stamped mark **$550**

Coppertone, perched frog and lily pads, and flower frog, marked in script,
2-1/4" x 11". . . . .**$450-$650**

Coppertone, flaring, paper labels and incised mark, 3" x 13-1/2" dia
. . . .**$300-$400**

Coppertone, frog perched on lily pads, stamped mark, 4-1/4" x 11"
. . . .**$300-$500**

Coppertone, has two squared, ribbed handles on the flat rim, incised mark,
5" x 7-1/2". . . . .**$250-$350**

Coppertone, frog perched on the side, stamped mark, 5" x 10". . .**$500-$800**

Coppertone, flaring, incised mark, 5" x 10-1/4". . . . .**$200-$300**

Dupont, decorated with birds on a wire between puffy green trees,
unmarked, 3-3/4" x 8" . . . .**$75-$150**

Fru Russett, squat, with berries and leaves on a blue ground, 6-1/2" dia
. . . .**$500-$700**

Glendale, large, flaring, embossed with birds and waves crashing over rocks,
stamped mark, 3" x 15" . . . .**$350-$500**

Greora, flaring, etched mark, 2-1/2" x 14-1/2". . . . .**$200-$300**

LaSa, low, painted with a landscape, unmarked, 9" dia . . . .**$200-$300**

Matt Green, embossed with dragonflies, unmarked, 3-3/4" x 7-1/2"
. . . .**$400-$600**

Matt Green, low, banded grapevine pattern, 9-1/4" dia . . . .**$500-$700**

Sicard, or ashtray, circular, buttressed, decorated with clover blossoms,
marked Weller on body, 2-1/2" x 6-1/2" . . . .**$450-$650**

Pumila, large, brown, 12" dia. . . . .**$150-$250**

Pumila, small, green, 8-1/2" dia . . . .**$100-$200**

Roma, footed, decorated with garlands and a medallion with bird,
unmarked, 5-1/4" x 11" . . . .**$75-$150**

Rosemont, low, pink Glasgow rose design, impressed mark, 9" dia **$50-$100**

Souevo, 4" . . . .**$50-$100**

Turada, corseted, impressed mark, 3-1/4" x 8" . . . .**$150-$250**

Woodcraft, with panels of squirrels in the forest, stamped mark, 6" dia
. . . .**$150-$250**

Turtle bowl with built-in flower frog, Muskota, unmarked, 4" x 9"
. . . .**$500-$1,000**

Candlestick

Blue Drapery, pair, stamped marks, 9-1/2" h . . . .**$100-$200**

Glendale, owl dec, 13-1/2" h **$520**

Rosemont, pair, glossy black with banded red floral design, impressed mark,
8-3/4". . . . .**$200-$400**

Sicard, with stars and butterflies decoration, marked on body, 6-1/2"
. . . .**$600-$800**

Clock, Louwelsa, painted with yellow lilies, signed with artist's initials, 6"
. . . .**$300-$500**

Console set

Glendale, consisting of a flaring bowl, a flower frog, and a pair of
candlesticks, all marked, bowl 15" diameter . . . .**$400-$700**

Tutone, pr candlesticks, green, stamped marks, 3-1/2" h, and 7" d
three-sided bowl. **$250**

Cookie jar, Mammy, marked "Weller Pottery since 1872," 11-1/2" x 7"
. . . .**$1,250-$1,750**

Dish

Camelot, yellow, footed, 8" . . . .**$500-$700**

Coppertone, frog perched along the edge, incised mark, 3" x 6-1/4"
. . . .**$250-$350**

Ewer

Aurelian, ruffled rim, painted by T.J. Wheatley with nasturtium, 10"
. . . .**$500-$700**

Aurelian, painted with orange carnations, impressed Aurelian mark, 11-1/2"
. . . .**$400-$600**

Dickensware II, decorated with ducks along the bank of a river, incised mark
with numbers, 9" x 6" . . . .**$400-$600**

Dickensware II, extremely rare and unusual, carved, shows a golfer and
caddy along a deeply incised line of trees. It is one of the finest examples
of a golfer I've seen, and would have sold for a considerable amount had
this decoration been found on a vase form, with artist's signature (which
it lacked). Impressed mark, 11" x 5". . . . .**$3,000-$4,000**

Dickensware II, decorated with mallards along a riverbank, impressed mark
3280, 13" x 5". . . . .**$500-$700**

Jap Birdimal, squeezebag trees and geisha dec by Rhead, incised mark
. . . .**$3,000**

Louwelsa, squat, ruffled rim, painted with gold and brown nasturtium,
impressed mark, 6-1/2" x 5-1/2" . . . .**$175-$275**

Louwelsa, squat, painted with a rose, impressed mark, 4-1/2" x 5-1/2"
. . . .**$200-$300**

Matt Floretta, incised with pears on a branch, incised mark, 10-1/2" x 4-1/2"
. . . .**$250-$350**

Figure

Brighton, pheasant, unmarked, 5" x 7". . . . .**$400-$600**

Brighton, parrot on a perch, large size, impressed WELLER, 7-1/4" x 5-1/2"
. . . .**$750-$1,000**

Coppertone, "Banjo Frog," 9". . . . .**$4,000-$5,000**

Coppertone, dancing frogs, extremely rare, 16-1/2". . . . . . .**$7,000-$9,000**

Coppertone, frog, stamped mark, 2-1/4" x 2-1/2" . . . .**$150-$250**

Coppertone, frog, 3-3/4". . . . .**$200-$300**

Coppertone, frog, unmarked, 6" x 7-1/4" . . . .**$500-$750**

Coppertone, turtle, unmarked, 2-1/2" x 6" . . . .**$350-$550**

Coppertone, turtle, unmarked, 2-1/2" x 6-1/2" . . . .**$250-$350**

Graystone Garden Ware, dog, large, black and white, incised mark,
12" x 11-1/2" . . . .**$2,000-$3,000**

Graystone Garden Ware, hen with chicks, colorful, incised mark, 8"
. . . .**$2,000-$3,000**

Graystone Garden Ware, pelican, large and very rare, unmarked, 20" x 17"
. . . .**$4,000-$6,000**

Muskota or Flemish, little girl with a watering can, unmarked, 6-1/2" x 4"
. . . .**$500-$750**

Muskota/Flemish, woman kneeling on rocks, unmarked, 7". . . . .**$350-$500**

Fish bowl holder

Flemish, shows fishing boy, 12"..............................$750-$1,000

Muskota, playing cat, impressed mark, 10" x 11"............$1,750-$2,750

Muskota, playful cat figure and trunk-shaped bud vase (sometimes seen fitted as a lamp), impressed mark, 11" x 11-1/4"...........$1,250-$1,750

Flower frog, Brighton, bright blue kingfisher, unmarked, 3-1/2", **$100-$200**.

Flower frog

Brighton, bright blue kingfisher, unmarked, 3-1/2" ....$100-$200

Brighton, with two small yellow birds perched on branches, unmarked, 4-1/2" x 4"..$350-$450

Brighton (sometimes attributed to the Muskota line), two-duck flower frog, 5-1/2"..$300-$500

Brighton, with two swans, impressed mark, 6" x 9".............$600-$800

Brighton, flying blue bird and apple tree, unmarked, 9"........$750-$1,000

Hobart, with child and duck, impressed mark, 5" x 4-1/2" ....$100-$200

Muskota, figure of a boy fishing, unmarked, 7" x 5" ....$250-$350

Muskota, with chicks, a rare example with holes for flowers, 5-1/2" x 4-1/2"
....$600-$800

Muskota, crab, impressed mark, 11-1/2" x 5"...................$100-$200

Muskota, frog on rock, impressed WELLER, 3-1/2" x 5-1/2" ......$300-$500

Muskota, shaped as a frog perched on a rock, impressed mark, 3-3/4" x 5-1/4"..$400-$600

Muskota, frog on a white water lily, impressed mark, 5" x 4-3/4"..$200-$300

Muskota, lobster, impressed mark, 1-1/2" x 6" ....$250-$350

Muskota, swan, unmarked, 2-1/2" x 5-1/2".....................$300-$500

Muskota, turtle, 4" x 5".......................................$200-$400

Muskota, with a nude figure seated on rocks, 8"................$450-$750

Fountain, Flemish, large fishing boy, incised mark, 20".......**$2,000-$3,000**

Fountain frog

Coppertone, stamped mark, 8-1/2" x 10"...................$1,500-$2,500

Graystone Garden Ware, covered in a fine yellow, brown, and pale green mottled glaze, unmarked, 10" x 11".......................$1,500-$2,500

Frog tray, oval, raised edge, frog and water lily on one side, lily pads on other, blotchy semi-gloss green glaze, "Weller Pottery" ink stamp, 15-1/2" l .$635

Garden ornament

Pop-Eye dog, large, marked in script, 10-1/2" x 8-1/2".......**$3,000-$4,000**

Swan, ivory glaze, minor flakes, 20" x 18" $6,500

Hair receiver

Jap Birdimal, or squat vessel, closed-in rim, painted by Hattie Ross with Viking ships, artist's initials, 1-3/4" x 3-3/4"..................$350-$550

Jap Birdimal, decorated with Viking ships, 2" x 4" ....$400-$600

Hanging basket

Forest, unmarked, 7-3/4" x 3-1/2" $300

Parian, conical, unmarked, 9-1/4" x 5-3/4" ....$100-$200

Woodcraft, large, with owls in a tree, 4-3/4" x 10" ....$200-$300

Woodcraft, with owls in an apple tree, 5" x 9-3/4"...............$300-$400

Humidor

Dickensware II Chinaman, incised mark, 6-1/4" x 6"..........$1,000-$1,500

Dickensware II, Turk etched mark, 7-1/4" x 6-1/2" ....$650-$950

Jar

Greora, covered, flaring, etched mark, 2-1/2" x 14-1/2"..........$200-$300

Selma, lidded, decorated with swans, impressed mark, 4-1/4"....$650-$950

Jardinière, Dickensware I, painted with roses on a purple ground, impressed mark, 10-1/2", **$300-$500**.

Jardinière

Aurelian, brown glaze, painted fruit, sgd "Frank Ferrell".............**$1,100**

Baldin, brown, impressed mark, 9" x 13".........................$350-$550

Burntwood, large, with roosters, impressed mark, 8-1/2" x 9-1/2".$250-$350

Cameo Jewell, impressed mark, 7-1/2" x 10".....................$300-$500

Clinton Ivory, panels of flowers, unmarked, 5" x 6" .... $50-$75

Clinton Ivory, rare, with squirrels, birds, and owls in trees, unmarked, 7" x 8"
....$400 $600

Dickensware I, painted with orange flowers, impressed mark, 8-1/2" x 11"
....$250-$350

Dickensware I, painted with roses on a purple ground, impressed mark, 10-1/2"..$300-$500

Dickensware I, painted with nasturtium on a dark green ground, impressed mark and illegible artist's cipher, 11-1/2" x 7-1/2" ....$300-$400

Eocean, pink carnations, unmarked, 7" x 8-1/2"..................$150-$250

Etched Floral/Matt, decorated with grapevines, unmarked, 7" x 9"
....$200-$300

Etched Floral/Matt, by Frank Ferrell with sunflowers in burnt orange on ivory over celadon ground, artist's signature, 10" x 13-1/2" $450-650

Flemish, decorated with colorful birds, leaves, and flowers, unmarked, 10-1/2" x 15"..$500-$700

Jardinière and pedestal set, Baldin, large, impressed mark, 40" overall, **$1,500-$2,000**.

Jardinière and pedestal set, Zona, rare, decorated with panels of cattails and kingfishers, stamped mark, 30-1/2", **$1,500-$2,500**.

Forest, impressed mark to both pieces, 28" overall . . . . **$1,000-$1,500**

Jap Birdimal, with cobalt trees under a full moon on a light blue ground, impressed mark, 11-1/2" x 13-1/2" . . . .**$450-$650**

Marvo, brown, stamped marked, 10" . . . .**$150-$250**

Matt Green, closed-in rim, unmarked, 7-3/4" x 10-1/2" . . . .**$200-$300**

Matt Green, embossed with Greek key pattern and buttresses, unmarked, 8-1/4" x 10-1/2" . . . .**$350-$500**

Matt Green, embossed, four handles styled as Arts & Crafts strap hardware, unmarked, 9-3/4" x 12" **$350-500**

Matt green, applied leaf handles, floriform feet, and embossed lilies, 15" x 15-1/2" . . . .**$750-$950**

Sicard, sunflowers, emerald green and gold on deep purple ground .**$2,900**

Sicard, large, decorated with sunflowers, marked in script, 10-1/2" x 12" . . . .**$2,000-$3,000**

Silvertone, has clusters of hydrangea, stamped mark, 11" x 10-1/2" . . . .**$600-$900**

Souevo, has a band of snail-like designs near the rim, unmarked, 7-1/4" x 9-1/4" . . . .**$200-$400**

Turada, massive with banded floral decoration in orange and ivory on an olive ground, impressed Turada 217 mark, 17" x 18" . . . .**$1,000-$1,500**

Woodcraft, rare, cats chasing birds through twisted vines and flowers, 7-3/4" x 9" . . . .**$750-$1,000**

Woodcraft, has a woodpecker perched on the side, 8" x 5-1/2" . . .**$400-$600**

Jardinière and pedestal set

Baldin, impressed mark, 38" overall . . . .**$1,000-$1,500**

Baldin, large, impressed mark, 40" overall . . . .**$1,500-$2,000**

Blue Drapery, unmarked, 29" overall . . . .**$600-$900**

Clinton Ivory, embossed with vines of roses, stamped mark, 24" overall . . . .**$500-$600**

Etna, painted with pink nasturtium, unmarked, 25-1/2" . . . .**$750-$1,000**

Flemish, with birds and flowers on an ivory ground, unmarked, 30" overall . . . .**$1,000-$2,000**

Flemish, stylized four-petaled red and green flowers on an ivory ground, 36" overall . . . .**$750-$1,000**

Marvo, brown, stamped mark, 32" overall . . . .**$750-$1,000**

Roma, 30" . . . .**$500-$750**

Zona, rare, decorated with panels of cattails and kingfishers, stamped mark, 30-1/2" . . . .**$1,500-$2,500**

Zona, columns and bands of flowers in polychrome, unmarked, 32-1/2" overall height . . . .**$650-$950**

Jug

Barcelona, Barcelonaware label, 6-1/2" x 5-1/2" . . . .**$100-$200**

Dickensware II by A.H., incised with a monk and painted with chains of flowers, impressed Dickensware Weller, artist's initials, 6" . . . . .**$350-$500**

Louwelsa, ruffled rim, painted with yellow flowers, impressed mark, 6" x 5" . . . .**$100-$200**

Louwelsa, squat, painted with oak branches, impressed mark, 3-1/4" x 5-3/4" . . . .**$150-$250**

Louwelsa, painted by Minnie Mitchell with cherries, impressed mark and artist's initials, 6" . . . .**$100-$200**

Lamp base, Dickensware II, incised with trees, no visible mark, 9-3/4", **$2,000-$3,000**.

Lamp base

Dickensware I, large, painted by C. J. Dibowski with large cactus blossoms in yellow and amber, complete with original oil lamp font, artist signed and impressed 350, pottery 17-1/2" x 12" . . . .**$650-$850**

Dickensware II, incised with trees, no visible mark, 9-3/4" . . . .**$2,000-$3,000**

Forest, unmarked, 2" chip next to hole at base, 5" d, 11-1/4" h **$460**

Louwelsa, by Hattie Mitchell, gourd shape, painted yellow cherry blossoms, stamped "Weller Louwelsa," sgd "H. Mitchell" on body, 10" d, 13-1/4" h **$460**

Matt Green, formed with twisted leaves at base and blossoms around the rim, unmarked, 14-1/2" x 6" . . . .**$1,500-$2,500**

Sicard, bulbous, floral decoration, 15-1/2" . . . .**$2,000-$3,000**

Sicard, with heavy glaze drips and unusual sea life decoration, 15-1/2" . . . .**$2,000-$3,000**

Xenia, finely decorated with pink flowers on a matt deep green-blue ground, impressed mark, 14-1/4" . . . .**$1,500-$2,000**

Mug, Jap Birdimal, two-handles, decorated with a Viking ship in dark blue on a pale yellow-ivory ground, impressed mark, 4" x 6-1/4", **$200-$400**.

Mug, Jewell, large, with medallions of a woman and grapevines, the base decorated with a band of red jewels between twisted vines, 6-3/4" x 5-1/4", **$250-$350**.

Oil lamp base, Rhead Faience, decorated with a band of geese, 13-1/2" x 16-1/2", **$1,250-$1,750**.

Mug

Dickensware, dolphin handle and band, sgraffito ducks **$250**
Dickensware I, decorated in squeezebag with garlands of orange and yellow blossoms around rim and a fish scale pattern at base, against a dark green ground, impressed mark, 7" x 5-1/2" **$400-600**
Dickensware II, incised and painted by Anna Dautherty with Native American, "Blue Hawk," impressed mark and artist's initials, 5-1/2" x 5" . . . .**$250-$350**
Dickensware II, corseted with dolphin handle and molded, stylized band near rim, the body incised with swimming carp in polychrome on a blue and green ground, impressed mark, 6-1/2" x 4-1/4" . . . .**$300-$500**
Etched Matt, typical decoration, incised mark, 5" x 4-3/4" . . . .**$150-$250**
Jap Birdimal, two-handles, decorated with a Viking ship in dark blue on a pale yellow-ivory ground, impressed mark, 4" x 6-1/4" . . . .**$200-$400**
Jewell, large, with medallions of a woman and grapevines, the base decorated with a band of red jewels between twisted vines, 6-3/4" x 5-1/4" . . . .**$250-$350**
Louwelsa, finely painted with a portrait of a man, impressed mark, 6" x 5-3/4" . . . .**$400-$500**
Louwelsa, painted with a portrait of an Arabian man, impressed mark, 6-1/2" x 4-1/4" . . . .**$350-$450**
Louwelsa, painted by J. E. with gooseberries and leaves, impressed Louwelsa mark and artist's initials, 6-1/4" x 5-1/2" . . . .**$150-$250**
Louwelsa, painted with grapes, marked, 6-1/2" **$200**
Turada, twisted handle, Weller Turada mark, 6" . . . .**$75-$150**
Woodcraft, embossed with foxes in their den, impressed mark, 6" x 5-1/4" . . . .**$400-$600**

Oil lamp

Louwelsa, three-handled, footed, painted with berries, impressed mark. Pottery only: 7-1/4" x 10-3/4" . . . .**$300-$400**
Turada, three-footed, no visible mark, pottery is 7-3/4" . . . .**$450-$650**

Oil lamp base

Rhead Faience, decorated with a band of geese, 13-1/2" x 16-1/2" . . . .**$1,250-$1,750**

Pedestal

Aurelian, twisted, painted by Frank Ferrell with grapes, artist signed, 26" x 10-1/2" . . . .**$400-$600**
Aurelian, twisted, painted with palm fronds, unmarked, 26" x 10-1/2" . . . .**$300-$500**
Jap Birdimal, with cobalt trees against a line blue ground, unmarked, 16-1/2" . . . .**$500-$750**
Louwelsa, painted by Eugene Roberts with blackberries and branches, impressed mark and artist's initials, 23" . . . .**$300-$500**

Pitcher

Aurelian, squat, painted with small orange flowers and green leaves, impressed mark, 5-1/2" x 5-3/4" . . . .**$200-$300**
Coppertone, bulbous, fish handle, stamped mark, 8" x 8" . . . .**$1,500-$2,500**
Dickensware II, small, incised with portrait of a Native American on a tan and green ground, 4" x 3-3/4" . . . .**$350-$500**
Dickensware II, tall, "Captain Duttle Gives Them The Lovely Pea," stamped mark, 12-1/2" x 7" . . . .**$450-$650**
Louwelsa, painted with grapes, marked, 12-1/2" . . . .**$150-$200**
Marvo, pink, unmarked, 8" x 8" . . . .**$250-$350**
Woodcraft, tall, shows foxes in their den, impressed mark, 12-1/2" x 7-1/2" . . . .**$750-$1,000**
Zona, shows ducks splashing in puddles, impressed mark, 7-1/2" x 7" . . . .**$150-$250**
Zona, with lightly colored panels of kingfishers and cattails, impressed mark, 8-1/2" x 9" . . . .**$150-$250**

Pitcher, Dickensware II, small, incised with portrait of a Native American on a tan and green ground, 4" x 3-3/4", **$350-$500**.

Planter

Baldin, blue, unmarked, 4-1/4" x 8"............................$200-$300

Baldin, brown, squat, impressed mark, 6" x 6-1/2"...............$200-$300

Blue Ware, footed, with maidens in yellow dresses, unmarked,
7-1/4" x 8"..$200-$300

Flemish, covered in oak leaves, 9-1/2" x 10-1/2"................$400-$600

Flemish, footed, band of leaves and fruit, unmarked, 10-1/2" x 12"
....$250-$350

Knifewood, fine and carved with bluebirds in an apple tree, unmarked,
6" x 7"...$750-$1,250

Matt Green, rare, architectural form, ribbed bands to body and buttressed
handles, unmarked, 7" x 10"...................................$650-$950

Muskota, turtle, with attached water lily flower frog, 4-1/2" x 9" ..$350-$500

Patricia, duck form, covered in an Evergreen glaze, incised mark, 8" x 16"
....$150-$250

Roma, large ovoid with clusters of red roses, unmarked, 5-1/2" x 16"
....$300-$400

Roma, faceted, unmarked, 6-1/2" x 7"............................$75-$150

Rosemont, unmarked, 7-1/2" x 9-1/2".............................$600-$800

Selma, painted with birds in fruit trees, impressed mark, 6" x 6-1/2"
....$500-$750

Warwick, two-handled, impressed mark, 4-1/2" x 9-3/4".........$75-$150

Woodcraft, applied squirrel climbing up tree, 2" tight line $375

Woodcraft, with daffodils and mushrooms, impressed mark, 5-1/2" x 10"
....$350-$500

Woodcraft, cylindrical, decorated with foxes in their den, unmarked 6" x 7"
....$300-$500

Woodcraft, large and rare, woodpecker perched on the side, unmarked,
8" x 11"..$600-$800

Plates

Burntwood, large, decorated with swimming fish, unmarked, 12" dia.
....$450-$650

Zona, lunch and dinner, some with stamped mark, 7-1/2" and 9" dia.
....$30-$50 each

Zona, two serving plates, both with stamp mark, 9-3/4" .... $50-$100 each

Potpourri jar, Warwick, lidded, 5"..........................$200-$250

Tankard, Woodcraft, embossed with foxes in their den, impressed mark,
13" x 7"...$800-$1,200

Two serving plates, Zona, both with stamp mark, 9-3/4", **$50-$100 each**.

Tea pot, Rhead Faience, decorated by L. P. with a panoramic village landscape in indigo on a blue-green ground, embossed Weller 3047/artist's
initials, label from White Pillars museum, 5-3/4" x 9"........**$800-$1,200**

Tobacco jar, Creamware, lidded, embossed with pipes and flowers,
unmarked, 7-1/2" x 5-1/2" ....$200-$300

Umbrella stand

Baldin, brown, unmarked....................................**$1,000-$1,750**

Bedford Matt, covered in the standard matt green glaze, unmarked, 20"
....**$600-$900**

Cameo Jewell, shaded gray ground, 22-1/2"..................**$750-$1,000**

Cameo Jewell, impressed mark, 22-1/2".....................**$1,000-$2,000**

Clinton Ivory, with stylized leaves, unmarked, 20" ....$200-$400

Clinton Ivory, impressed mark, 20-1/2".........................$200-$300

Clinton Ivory, unmarked, 22-1/2" x 10" ....$500-$750

Flemish, decorated with maidens, chains of pink flowers, and ivy, impressed
mark, 20"...**$750-$1,250**

Flemish, unmarked, 20-1/2" x 10-3/4" ....$500-$700

Flemish, unmarked, 22" x 10-1/2" ....$400-$600

Forest, 22"...**$1,000-$1,500**

Marvo, green, ink stamp and paper label, 19-1/2" x 11" ....$750-$950

Marvo, covered in an orange glaze, stamped mark, 20"........$750-$1,000

Matt Green, embossed with geometric floral pattern, unmarked,
20" x 10"..$600-$800

Rhead, decorated with swimming ducks, and squirrels in trees, extremely
unusual, 19" x 14 ....**$6,000-$8,000**

Umbrella
stand, Rhead,
decorated with
swimming ducks,
and squirrels in
trees, extremely
unusual, 19" x 14,
$6,000-$8,000.

Vase

Ardsley, flaring, with cattails and water lilies, stamped mark, 9" x 3-3/4"
....**$100-$200**

Ardsley, flaring, stamped mark, 10-1/2" x 7-1/2" ....**$250-$350**

Ardsley, decorated with irises, 9-1/2" x 5-1/4"...................**$350-$500**

Ardsley, with stepped base, stamped mark, 10" x 5-1/4".........**$300-$500**

Athens, with mythological medallions, 9-3/4" x 6", unmarked ..**$750-$1,000**

Atlas, flaring, in blue and ivory, script mark, 6" x 9-1/4"..........**$200-$300**

Aurelian, classically shaped, painted with blossoms and berries, incised
  mark and illegible artist's initials, 10-1/4" x 4" ....**$350-$550**

Aurelian, singing monk playing the mandolin in earthtone glazes, mkd
  "Aurelian" on base, numbered, decorator's signature for R. G. Turner on
  side, crazing, c1904, 19" h.......................................**$1,530**

Aurelian, ovoid, painted by Frank Ferrell with poppies, incised mark,
  stamped mark, and artist's initials, 17".....................**$750-$1,250**

Aurelian, tall ovoid, finely painted by R. G. Turner with a full-figure portrait
  of monk, incised mark, artist's signature, 19" x 6-3/4".....**$1,500-$2,000**

Aurelian, tapered, finely painted with berries and leaves, impressed mark,
  9-1/2" x 4"..**$250-$350**

Aurelian, tapering, berries and leaves, imp mark, 9-1/2" h, 4" d **$300**

Auroro, has daisies on a pale blue ground, marked in script, 8" x 4"
  .... **$750-$1,000**

Auroro, undecorated other than the shaded blue background, incised mark,
  6-1/2"..**$500-$700**

Auroro, light blue, ovoid, incised mark, 9" ....**$800-$1,200**

Auroro-type, very finely decorated in unusual colors, 9-1/4" .**$3,000-$4,000**

Baldin, blue, bulbous, unmarked, 7-1/4" x 6".....................**$150-$250**

Baldin, brown bulbous with two branch handles, impressed mark, 9" x 8"
  ....**$400-$600**

Baldin, blue, bulbous, two branch handles, impressed mark, 9" x 8-1/2"
  ....**$450-$650**

Baldin, blue, imp mark, glaze nick at rim, 9" h, 9" d....................**$475**

Baldin, blue, tapered, impressed mark, 13" x 6-1/2" ....**$400-$600**

Baldin, brown, tapered, impressed mark, 13" x 7-1/2"............**$450-$650**

Baldin, blue, tapered, impressed mark, 13" x 7-1/2" ....**$500-$700**

Barcelona, large baluster, stamped Barcelona Weller, Barcelonaware paper
  label, 11"..**$300-$400**

Vase, Blue and Decorated, tear-shaped, found with a very rare banded peacock feather design, marked WELLER, 9", **$2,500-$3,500**.

Double wall vase, Brighton, kingfisher decoration, unmarked, 12" x 5-1/2", **$750-$1,000**.

Barcelona, bulbous, stamped mark, 11" x 6-1/4" ....**$200-$300**

Barcelona, tall corseted, buttressed handles, 14", unmarked .....**$500-$800**

Besline, bulbous, decorated with berries and leaves on a lustred orange
  ground, unmarked, 8-1/2" x 6" ....**$350-$500**

Blo' Red, ovoid, covered in bright orange mottled glaze, 9" x 4"...**$200-$300**

Blue and Decorated, tear-shaped, found with a very rare banded peacock
  feather design, marked WELLER, 9".......................**$2,500-$3,500**

Blue and Decorated, painted with yellow, pink, and ivory pansies, impressed
  mark, 10" x 5-1/4"...**$250-$350**

Blue and Decorated, faceted, painted with a bluebird and cherry blossoms,
  impressed mark, 11-1/2" x 5"............................**$1,000-$1,500**

Blue and Decorated, tapering, painted with berries and leaves, impressed
  mark, 13-1/2" x 4-1/4".......................................**$300-$400**

Blue and Decorated Hudson, tear-shaped, painted with white roses,
  impressed mark, 9"..**$300-$400**

Blue and Decorated Hudson, faceted, painted with a band of pink and white
  peonies, impressed mark, 11-1/2" x 5".......................**$250-$350**

Blue Ware, ovoid, with maiden in yellow dress, impressed mark, 7-1/4" x
  3-3/4"...**$150-$250**

Blue Ware, ovoid, features a maiden playing an instrument, unmarked,
  8-1/2" x 3-1/2"..**$150-$250**

Blue Ware, flaring, impressed mark, 8-3/4" x 4-1/2"..............**$150-$250**

Blue Ware, large, has maidens dancing and playing instruments, stamped
  mark, 12" x 6-1/2"...**$300-$400**

Bonito, bulbous, painted with pink daisies, marked in script, 6" x 5-1/4"
  ....**$75-$150**

Bonito, bulbous, painted with tulips, marked in script, 7-1/2" x 4-1/2"
  ....**$100-$150**

Bonito, ovoid, two handles, painted with pink and amber columbine,
  marked in script, 11" x 5-1/2"...............................**$200-$300**

Brighton, double wall, kingfisher decoration, unmarked, 12" x 5-1/2"
  ....**$750-$1,000**

Bronze Ware, ovoid, using a Drapery mold, covered in a bronze feathered
  glaze, stamped mark, 9-1/2" x 4-3/4" ....**$400-$600**

Bronze Ware, tall, curdled reddish bronze glaze, unmarked, 13"..**$600-$800**

Bronze Ware, baluster, tall, unmarked, 13-3/4" x 7"..........**$1,000-$1,500**

Burntwood, bulbous, band of flowers, unmarked, 4-1/4" h, 3-3/4" d **$100**

Burntwood, bulbous, with a band of flowers, unmarked, 3-3/4" x 4-1/4"
  ....**$50-$100**

Vase, Chase, bulbous, incised mark, 10" x 7-1/2", **$300-$400**.

Burntwood, cylindrical, crisply decorated with figures, unmarked, 8" x 4"
....**$250-$350**

Burntwood, cylindrical, decorated with Egyptian figures, paper label, 9-1/2"
....**$300-$400**

Camelot, large bulbous, yellow and white, unmarked, 8-1/2".**$1,000-$2,000**

Camelot, corseted, gray-green and white, unmarked, 11-1/2"**$1,000-$2,000**

Camelot, large and rare, unmarked, 12" x 5-1/2" ....**$2,000-$2,500**

Chase, bulbous, marked in script, 8" x 5"......................**$300-$400**

Chase, bulbous, incised mark, 10" x 7-1/2".....................**$300-$400**

Chengtu, faceted, stamped mark, 9-1/4" x 4" ....**$200-$300**

Claywood, flaring with butterflies, unmarked, 3" x 3-1/4"........**$150-$250**

Claywood, with swimming ducks, unmarked, 3" x 3-1/4"........**$150-$250**

Claywood, squat with banded floral design, unmarked, 3-3/4" x 4-1/2"
....**$150-$250**

Clinton Ivory, cylindrical, with rows of oak leaves, unmarked, 9-1/4" x 4-1/2"
....**$75-$150**

Clinton Ivory, ovoid, embossed with squirrels and leafy branches, unmarked,
11-1/2" x 5"...**$450-$650**

Cloudburst, bud, corseted, red, unmarked, 6"....................**$100-$150**

Cloudburst, bud, trumpet-shaped, Weller Ware sticker, 9".......**$250-$400**

Cloudburst, ovoid, in brown, orange, and ivory, unmarked, 10-1/2" x 4"
....**$300-$400**

Coppertone, double vase, formed by two jumping fish, impressed mark,
8-1/2"...**$1,500-$2,500**

Coppertone, spherical, incised "E," 7" x 8-1/2" ....**$300-$400**

Coppertone, bulbous with a frog perched on the rim, unmarked, 7-1/2" x 7"
....**$1,250-$1,750**

Coppertone, bulbous, two frogs perched on the side, the body embossed
with leaves, stamped mark, 7-3/4" x 8-1/2"................**$1,000-$1,500**

Coppertone, pillow, flaring, two frogs perched on the squat base, stamped
mark, 8-1/4" x 9-1/4"....................................**$1,000-$1,500**

Copra, flaring, painted with berries, blossoms, and leaves, impressed mark,
8" x 5-1/2"...**$150-$250**

Copra, flaring, ring handles, painted with ivory and pink poppies, impressed
mark, 10" x 7"...**$350-$450**

Cornish, blue, corseted, marked in script, 7-1/4" x 4-1/4" ....**$100-$200**

Cretone, bulbous, black decoration on an ivory ground, marked in script,
artist's initials MT, 6-3/4" x 7" ....**$600-$800**

Cretone, black, bulbous, with flowers and animals in ivory, signed Hester
Pillsbury and incised mark, 7"...............................**$700-$900**

Cretone, yellow matte glaze, decoration in brown, marked in script, 8-1/4"
....**$600-$900**

Dickensware I, bulbous, beautifully decorated by Frank Ferrell with chrysanthemums in polychrome, impressed mark and signed Ferrell,
7" x 6-1/2"...**$1,500-$2,500**

Dickensware I, four-sided, incised and painted with tulips and yellow
scrolled design, impressed 672, 9-1/4" x 6"....................**$450-$650**

Dickensware I, four-sided, incised and painted with tulips and yellow
scrolled design, impressed 672, 9-1/4" x 6"....................**$450-$650**

Dickensware I, tall baluster, finely painted by Frank Ferrell with clusters of
blue and yellow hydrangea, impressed mark, signed Ferrell, 13-1/2" x
6-1/4"..**$1,500-$2,500**

Dickensware II, bell shaped and high glaze, decorated with a scene from the
"Pickwick Papers," impressed numbers, 12-1/4" x 8-1/4" ...**$1,000-$1,500**

Dickensware II, bulbous, incised and painted with an Indian chief on a
robin's egg blue ground, impressed mark, 9" ....**$1,500-$2,000**

Dickensware II, bulbous, exceptionally decorated by Carl Weigelt with a
classical scene, impressed mark and artist's initials, 10"....**$1,500-$2,500**

Dickensware II, corseted, decorated with a lady golfer, signed KP, 10-1/2"
....**$1,500-$2,000**

Dickensware II, cylindrical, shows male golfer in mid-swing, crisply carved
and detailed, impressed mark, 9-1/4" x 3-1/4".............**$1,500-$2,500**

Dickensware II, pillow, incised and painted with a mallard on a shore, very
similar to a Hunter piece in matt glaze, impressed mark and several
artist's marks including Charles Upjohn, 5" x 5-1/2" ....**$400-$600**

Dickensware III, bell-shaped, painted with figure of a man, "Mr. Weller Sr,"
signed and stamped, 8-1/4" x 7-1/4".......................**$750-$1,000**

Dresden, tall cylindrical, painted by Levi Burgess with a panoramic Delft
scene, signed LJB, stamped Weller Matt, 16" x 4-1/2"........**$500-$750**

Elberta, large bulbous, marked in script, 10" x 10"...............**$400-$600**

Eocean, with buttressed rim, beautifully painted by Mae Timberlake with
grapes on a vine, marked in script and artist's initials, 12-3/4" x 5"
....**$750-$1,000**

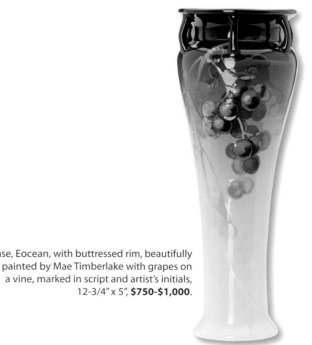

Vase, Eocean, with buttressed rim, beautifully painted by Mae Timberlake with grapes on a vine, marked in script and artist's initials, 12-3/4" x 5", **$750-$1,000**.

Eocean, fine and tall cylindrical, beautifully painted by Eugene Roberts with pink and ivory thistle, incised mark and artist's initials, 20-1/2" x 5-3/4" ....**$2,500-$3,000**

Eocean, short rim on cylindrical form, thistle plants in pink, maroon, and cream, green stems on brown to green to cream-colored ground, incised "Eocean Rose Weller," numbered "547," letter "Y" on base, artist's initials on side for Eugene Roberts, crazing and areas of glaze roughness, c1907, 21" h...**$1,880**

Eocean, bulbous, painted by Elizabeth Blake with a portrait of a kitten, incised mark and artist's signature, 8" x 4-1/4" ....**$1,500-$2,000**

Eocean, bulbous, painted with red berries and leaves, impressed mark, 8-1/2" x 5"...**$350-$500**

Eocean, ovoid, painted with dogwood, incised mark and unknown artist's mark, 9-1/2" x 4-1/4"...**$500-$700**

Eocean, painted with grapevines on a pale shaded gray-green ground, incised mark, 11-3/4" x 6-1/2" ....**$750-$1,250**

Eocean, finely painted with purple sweet peas on a teal to gray shaded ground, incised mark, 12"...................................**$650-$950**

Eocean, bulbous, painted with deep pink Clematis, incised mark, 13-1/4" x 7-1/2"...**$500-$700**

Eocean, tall, finely painted by Hester Pillsbury with pink orchids on an unusual shaded pink ground, incised mark and artist's mark, 15-1/2" x 6-1/2" ....**$2,000-$3,000**

Etched Floral/Matte, corseted, decorated with branches of berries and leaves on an orange ground, impressed mark, 10-3/4" x 4" ....**$350-$450**

Etched Floral/Matt, bulbous, decorated with yellow roses on an orange ground, impressed mark, 6-1/2" x 4-3/4".....................**$350-$450**

Etched Floral/Matt, four sided with raised rim carved with mushrooms in white on an orange ground, impressed mark, 7"..............**$300-$400**

Etched Floral/Matt, four-sided, carved and painted with red and yellow tulips on an ivory ground, impressed mark, 8"................**$300-$400**

Etched Floral/Matt, corseted, with berries, branches, and leaves on an ochre matt ground, unmarked, 13" x 4"...........................**$350-$500**

Etna, tapering, decorated with blue blossoms, impressed mark, 5-3/4" x 2-1/2"...**$75-$125**

Vase, Etna, molded with pink daisies against a shaded dark gray ground, 10-3/4" x 4-1/2", **$200-$300**.

Etna, molded with pink daisies against a shaded dark gray ground, 10-3/4" x 4-1/2"...**$200-$300**

Etna, gourd-shaped, painted with pink flowers, impressed Etna mark, 6-1/2" x 5-1/4" ....**$150-$250**

Etna, ovoid, painted with purple flowers, unmarked, 7" x 3-3/4"..**$200-$300**

Etna, classically shaped, with pink roses, impressed mark, 10-1/4" x 4" ....**$250-$350**

Etna, painted with tall daffodils, signed Weller on body and incised mark to base, 11-1/4" x 4-1/2" ....**$350-$450**

Etna, embossed with a portrait of Shakespeare and several jeweled accents, incised mark, 12"...**$800-$1,200**

Flemish, cylindrical, has a red rose "tied-on" by a blue ribbon, impressed mark, 8-3/4" x 2-1/2"...**$100-$200**

Floretta, three-sided with grapes, impressed mark, 7" x 3-1/2"....**$100-$150**

Floretta, cylindrical, with clusters of grapes, impressed mark, 9" x 3-1/4" ....**$50-$100**

Floretta, large, bulbous, decorated with clusters of grapes, impressed Floretta mark, 12" x 8"...................................**$200-$300**

Forest, flaring, unmarked, 7-3/4" x 5-1/2".....................**$150-$250**

Forest, slightly corseted, this example has crisp decoration, impressed mark, 8" x 4"...**$150-$300**

Frosted Matt, bulbous with flaring rim, covered in a heavily curdled bright green over mottled brown glaze, unmarked, 5-1/4" x 4-1/2"...**$300-$400**

Frosted Matt, baluster, in feathered green and gold glaze, unmarked, 12" x 6"...**$500-$700**

Frosted Matt, baluster, with heavily curdled pale lime green over sheer brown glaze, 13-1/2"...................................**$1,500-$2,500**

Frosted Matt, corseted, thick green curdled glaze, unmarked ....**$300-$500**

Fruitone, squat, two-handled, impressed WELLER, 5-1/4" ....**$350-$500**

Fruitone, large squat, unmarked, 5-1/2" x 7-1/4"................**$650-$950**

Fruitone, cylindrical, impressed WELLER, 8-3/4".................**$600-$900**

Fru Russet, emb flowers, pale blue-gray and green glaze, imp mark, 14" h, 5-3/4"...**$2,600**

Fru Russet, squat, decorated with white blossoms and leaves on one side, blue berries and leaves on the other, all on a mottled green ground, impressed mark, 3-1/2" x 5-1/2".........................**$1,000-$1,500**

Fru Russet, embossed with a salamander and covered in raspberry matte glaze, impressed mark, 4-3/4" x 3".......................**$1,000-$1,500**

Fru Russet, tapered, embossed with brown scarabs and red acanthus leaves on a blue and green ground, incised mark, 5" x 4-3/4".....**$2,000-$3,000**

Fru Russet, thick curdled glaze, impressed numbers on bottom, 7-1/2" ....**$500-$750**

Fru Russet, embossed with a bat and full moon hidden behind clouds, incised mark on body and impressed mark to underside, 8-1/2" x 7-1/2" ....**$2,000-$2,500**

Fudzi, corseted, decorated with sunflowers, one of the very few known marked examples of this line, impressed mark, 8-1/2".....**$1,000-$1,500**

Fudzi, ovoid, leaves and berries around the rim, impressed numbers, 10-1/2" ....**$1,500-$2,000**

Geode, bulbous, ivory, painted shooting star design in blue, incised mark, 3-3/4" x 4-1/2"...**$500-$700**

Geode, bulbous, white stars on a blue ground, 5-1/2"...........**$650-$950**

Glendale, double bud, embossed with a bluebird, nest, and berries, unmarked, 6-1/2" ....**$300-$400**

Glendale, baluster, embossed with birds, flowers, and butterflies, 12" ....**$750-$1,000**

Glendale, bulbous, decorated with a bird in flight, stamped mark, 7" x 4-1/4" ....**$350-$550**

Glendale, bulbous, covered in pink and green matt glaze, unmarked, 7" x 5"
....$250-$350
Glendale, ovoid, embossed with birds in their nest, unmarked, 8-1/4" x 4"
....$650-$950
Glendale, ovoid, embossed with three yellow birds on a branch, unmarked,
9" x 4" ....$600-$900
Glendale, ovoid, embossed with a bird and cattails, stamped mark,
13" x 6-1/4" ....$1,000-$1,500
Graystone Garden Ware, large, two handles, embossed with a wreath of
laurel leaves, stamp mark, 15-1/2" x 13"..................$400-$600
Greenaways, floor vase or umbrella stand, incised S. A. Weller, 22"
....$1,500-$2,500
Greora, bulbous with stepped body, the embossed floral band very crisp,
unmarked, 9"...$250-$500
Greora, corseted with wide rim, unmarked, 6-1/2" x 5-1/4"......$150-$250
Greora, divided fan, marked in script, 7" x 7"....................$250-$350
Greora, flaring, incised mark & Greora Ware label, 8-1/2" x 5-3/4" .$350-$500
Greora, flaring, etched mark, 11-1/2" h, 7" d $450
Greora, goblet-shaped, 9" ....$300-$500
Hudson, bulbous, painted band of white blossoms and leaves, Timberlake,
stamped mark, artist's signature, 6-3/4" h, 6-1/2" h.................$500

Hudson, two-handled, finely painted by Mae Timberlake with pink wild
roses, stamped mark and artist's signature, 5-1/2" x 8" ......$750-$1,000
Hudson, bulbous, two angular handles with pink flowers, stamped mark
and illegible artist's signature, 6" x 5-1/2"...................$400-$600
Hudson, bulbous, angular handles, painted with berries and leaves,
stamped mark, 6" x 5-1/2"...................................$350-$500
Hudson, ovoid, painted by Hester Pillsbury with irises on a lavender to pink
ground, incised mark, artist's mark, 6-1/4" x 3-1/4"...........$450-$650
Hudson, gourd shaped, painted by Sarah Reid McLaughlin with pink and
white dogwood, etched mark and artist's signature, 6-1/2"....$350-$500
Hudson, bulbous, two-handled, painted by Mae Timberlake with blue
flowers on a shaded pink ground, stamped and impressed marks, artist's
signature, 6-1/2" x 5-1/2"...................................$400-$600

Two vases, Hudson, ovoid, one painted by Hester Pillsbury with daffodils,
the other by H.F. with pink nasturtium, 7" x 3-3/4", **$400-$600 each.**

Hudson, bulbous, painted pink tulips, imp mark, 10-1/2" h, 4-3/4" d **$425**
Hudson, trumpet shape, painted berries and leaves, imp mark, 11" h, 4" d
....**$400**
Hudson, ovoid, painted with pink Wisteria, impressed mark, 9" x 4-1/4"
....**$400-$600**
Hudson, painted by Ruth Axline with a branch of large yellow and pink
dogwood blossoms around the entire rim, impressed mark, 9" x 4-1/2"
....**$350-$500**
Hudson, large, finely painted by Claude Leffler with irises on both sides,
impressed mark and artist's mark, 15" x 7" ....**$3,000-$4,000**

Vase, Hudson painted by Ruth Axline with a branch of large yellow and
pink dogwood blossoms around the entire rim, impressed mark,
9" x 4-1/2", **$350-$500.**

Hudson, bulbous, two angular handles, painted by Sarah Timberlake with blue flowers around the rim, stamped mark, 6-1/2" x 5-1/2"...**$350-$500**

Hudson, ovoid, painted with blue and white dogwood blossoms, stamped mark, 6-3/4"..**$300-$400**

Hudson, bulbous, painted by Timberlake with a band of white blossoms and leaves, stamped mark and artist's signature, 6-3/4" x 6-1/2"...**$350-$500**

Hudson, extremely unusual and painted by Hester Pillsbury in shades of gray with a California pine tree in stormy landscape, incised mark and artist's signature, 7"....................................**$2,000-$3,000**

Hudson, tall tapering, painted by I.F. with berries and leaves, impressed mark and artist's initials, 12-1/2" x 3-3/4"......................**$400-$600**

Hudson, painted by Dorothy England with blue delphiniums, stamped mark, impressed mark and artist's signature, 12-1/2" x 6"....**$800-$1,200**

Hudson Gray, tall ovoid with collared rim, finely painted by Mae Timberlake with ivory thistle on a shaded olive ground, impressed mark and artist's signature, 13-1/2" x 4-3/4"....................**$1,500-$2,000**

Hudson, large bulbous, painted by McLaughlin with blue and white irises on a blue ground, incised mark and artist's signature, 15" x 7"
....**$2,000-$3,000**

Hudson, large, twisted handles, painted by McLaughlin with sprays of pink and white hydrangea, marked in script and artist's signature, 15-1/4" x 7"
....**$2,500-$3,500**

Hudson, tall, painted by Pillsbury with irises, artist signed and marked, 15-1/2"....................................**$2,500-$3,500**

Hudson Light, painted with pink clematis, impressed mark, 10" x 5"
....**$300-$400**

Vase, Hudson Light, painted with pink clematis, impressed mark, 10" x 5", **$300-$400**.

Hudson Light, pear shaped, painted with pink wild roses, impressed mark, 7-1/4" x 4-1/4"....................................**$300-$400**

Hudson Light, bulbous, painted with water lilies, impressed mark, 8"..**$300-$400**

Hudson Light, cylindrical, painted with daffodils, impressed mark, 8-1/2" x 3-1/2"....................................**$300-$400**

Hudson Light, bulbous, painted with wild roses, impressed mark, 8-3/4" x 3-3/4"....................................**$350-$450**

Hudson Light, pear-shaped, painted with yellow and white irises, stamped mark, 11-1/2" x 5-1/2"....................................**$350-$500**

Hudson Light, faceted, painted with pink and white dogwood, impressed mark, 12" x 5-1/2"....................................**$250-$350**

Hudson Light, tall ovoid with collared rim, painted with pink thistle, impressed mark, 13-1/2" x 4-3/4"....................................**$400-$600**

Hudson Perfecto, glossy, bright blue, colorful bands of berries and leaves on a bright white ground, 6"....................................**$550-$750**

Hudson Perfecto, bulbous, painted by Hester Pillsbury with apple blossoms on a white to blue ground, impressed mark and artist's initials, 6" x 5"
....**$400-600**

Hudson Perfecto, bulbous, painted by Hester Pillsbury with a branch of pink flowers, impressed mark and artist's initials, 6" x 5-1/4"........**$350-$500**

Hudson Perfecto, tall, painted by Claude Leffler with flowers, marked with artist's signature....................................**$600-$800**

Hunter, pillow, painted with butterflies, incised mark and artist's initials, 5-1/4"....................................**$350-$500**

Hunter, rare, slightly flared, incised with seagulls flying over waves, marked with impressed numbers, 7-1/4" x 3"....................**$600-$900**

Jap Birdimal, matte green, decorated with circular red and yellow flowers, unmarked, 4" x 5"....................................**$800-$1,200**

Jap Birdimal, tapered, has swimming fish, marked with artist's initials UNH, 6-1/4" x 3-1/4"....................................**$800-$1,200**

Jap Birdimal, tapered, decorated with a geisha against a burnt orange ground, a crisply decorated and well articulated example of this line, artist-signed CMM, whose initials are often found on Jap Birdimal pieces, 7-1/2" x 3"....................................**$1,000-$1,500**

Jap Birdimal, three handles, bulbous, decorated in squeezebag by with stylized green, brown, and white trees on a teal blue ground, incised Weller Faience E500-1/2, artist signed OMN, 8-1/4" x 5-1/2".....**$1,500-$2,000**

Jewell, slightly tapered, decorated with peacock and jeweled feathers, impressed mark, 13" x 5-1/4"....................................**$1,000-$1,500**

Juneau, bright pink, impressed mark, 10"....................**$150-$250**

Kenova, with an applied turtle on the side, impressed mark, 5"..**$650-$950**

Kenova, two-handled, decorated with hanging branches of roses, unmarked, 10"....................................**$800-$1,200**

Knifewood, carved with butterflies and daisies, 4-1/4"..........**$300-$500**

Knifewood, decorated with swans and trees, impressed mark, 5" x 3-1/2"
....**$400-$600**

Knifewood, features squirrels, bluebirds, and hooded owls in a tree, impressed mark, 7" x 4"....................................**$1,000-$1,500**

Knifewood, ovoid, with daisies and butterflies all covered in matt glaze, impressed mark, 7" x 4-1/2"....................................**$350-$550**

Knifewood, fine and carved with hooded owls in a tree under a crescent moon, unmarked, 8-1/2" x 4-1/4"....................................**$750-$1,250**

L'Art Nouveau, pillow, one side with maiden in profile, other with shell, stamped mark partially obscured, 9-1/2" h, 8-1/2" w................**$450**

L'Art Nouveau, shell shape, painted maiden and flowers, imp mark, 1" line, two minor glaze flakes, 10" h, 8" d................................**$450**

L'Art Nouveau, with orange flowers and flowing leaves, 8-3/4"...**$300-$400**

L'Art Nouveau, shell-shaped, painted with maidens and flowers, impressed mark, 10" x 8-3/4"....................................**$500-$700**

L'Art Nouveau, four-sided, with panels of poppies and grapes, unmarked, 11" x 3-1/4"....................................**$350-$500**

L'Art Nouveau, bottle-shaped, orange flowers and spade-shaped leaves, unmarked, 13" x 5"....................................**$400-$600**

Lamar, bullet-shaped, painted with pine trees on a deep red ground, marked with several paper labels, 8-1/4"....................**$300-$500**

Lamar, cabinet, unmarked, 2-1/2" x 2-1/4"....................**$200-$300**

LaSa, bulbous, painted with swirling clouds by Frank Dedonatis with blue berries and orange leaves, artist's mark, 4" x 4-1/2".............**$300-$400**

LaSa, small ovoid, finely painted with clouds and trees, unmarked, 5" x 2-3/4"..**$500-$700**

LaSa, bullet-shaped, decorated with pine trees in front of a mountain and lake, unmarked, 6" x 3"......................................**$250-$350**

LaSa, pyramidal, painted with an evergreen tree and a lake landscape, marked on body, 6-1/4" x 1-3/4".............................**$300-$400**

Lonhuda, cabinet, classically shaped, painted by Albert Haubrich with delicate yellow blossoms on a green shaded ground, stamped mark and artist's initials, 5-1/4"..**$300-$400**

Lonhuda, three-footed, painted with gooseberries, impressed mark, 4-3/4" ....**$150-$250**

Louella, painted with irises, 9-1/2" ....**$150-$250**

Louwelsa, blue, ovoid, painted with delicate bluish blossoms, 8-1/2" x 3-3/4" ....**$850-$1,250**

Louwelsa, bulbous, orange and yellow carnations, imp mark, few short shallow scratches, 12" h, 3-1/4" h.............................**$100**

Louwelsa, gourd shaped, two handles, with gooseberry leaves, impressed mark, 5-1/2" x 4-1/2"......................................**$100-$200**

Louwelsa, ovoid, gooseberries and leaves, imp mark, fleck to rim, few shallow scratches, 10-1/2" h, 5-1/2" d.............................**$100**

Louwelsa, ovoid, finely painted by Levi Burgess with roses, impressed mark and artist's mark, 14-3/4" x 5"..........................**$250-$350**

Louwelsa, pillow, painted with wild roses, impressed mark, 4" x 5-1/4" ....**$150-$200**

Louwelsa, pillow, painted with orange poppies, unmarked, 5-1/2" x 5-1/2" ....**$150-$250**

Louwelsa, tall, two handles, painted by William Hall with nasturtium, stamped mark and artist's cipher, 15" x 5-1/4"................**$450-$650**

Louwelsa, vasiform body, yellow rose stems on brown ground, decorator's signature on side for Hattie Mitchell, imp maker's mark on base, numbered "466" and "1," minor glaze loss, c1900, 20-3/4" h............**$1,880**

Vase, Matt Green, basket-shaped, on a Silvertone blank, a crisply decorated example, 9" x 7-1/4", **$350-$550**.

Louwelsa, floor, painted by L. Mitchell with grape clusters, impressed mark and artist's signature, 18"...................................**$750-$1,000**

Louwelsa, tall cylindrical, finely painted by Turner with a portrait of Napoleon, 18" x 5".......................................**$1,250-$1,750**

Louwelsa, floor, rare, painted by E. Leffler with yellow roses on a shaded brown and lemon yellow ground, impressed mark and artist's signature, 28-1/4"..**$4,000-$5,000**

Lustre, unusual gold bulbous, Weller Ware and LP Ball Jeweler and Optometrist labels still intact, 3-3/4" x 4"....................**$100-$200**

Malverne, bulbous, unmarked, 5-1/2" ....**$75-$150**

Malverne, pillow, marked in script, 8" x 6" ....**$100-$200**

Manhattan, green with tall leaves, marked in script, 9" x 5".......**$100-$200**

Marengo, orange, faceted, 11-1/2"........................**$250-$350**

Matt Green, basket-shaped, on a Silvertone blank, a crisply decorated example, 9" x 7-1/4" ....**$350-$550**

Matt Green, twisted, impressed mark, 5-1/4" ....**$400-$600**

Matt Green, corseted, flat shoulder, this form also seen in the Camelot line, unmarked, 11-1/2"..................................**$850-$1,250**

Matt Green, tall, with banded handles, 12" ....**$1,500-$2,000**

Matt Green, corseted with reticulated rim and embossed poppy decoration, unmarked, 12-1/4" x 6-1/2"..............................**$1,500-$2,500**

Matt Green, unusual, with a molded band of apples around the rim, unmarked, 12-1/4" x 7"..................................**$1,200-$1,500**

Matt Green, large thistle blossoms and leaves, unmarked, 13-1/2" ....**$800-$1,200**

Matt Green, tall corseted with geometric design, unmarked, 15-1/2" ....**$300-$400**

Minerva, with amber trees, impressed mark, 13-1/2".........**$2,500-$3,500**

Neiska, blue bulbous with twisted handles, incised mark ....**$100-$200**

Pumila, brown, flaring, stamped mark, 10-1/4" x 6" ....**$150-$250**

Rhead Faience, bulbous, three-handled, painted with orange poppies on an olive ground, impressed 509, 8" x 7", ...**$1,250-$1,750**

Rhead Faience, bulbous, decorated in squeezebag with a band of walking ducks, and a geometric band around the rim, marked "Weller Rhead Faience", 8-3/4" x 6-1/4" ....**$2,500-$3,000**

Rochelle, painted by Claude Leffler with pink and yellow nasturtium, this example is extremely rare because Rochelle is rarely signed by anyone other than Pillsbury, 6-1/4"..................................**$400-$500**

Rochelle, bulbous, painted by Hester Pillsbury with blue and yellow flowers, incised mark and artist's initials, 6-1/2" x 3-1/4" ....**$700-$900**

Roma, buttressed, decorated with grapes, unmarked, 10" x 4-1/2" ....**$150-$250**

Roma, bottle shaped, 13-1/2"...................................**$200-$300**

Rosemont, bulbous, flaring rim, imp mark, 10" h, 4-1/2" d.............**$450**

Rosemont, classically shaped, decorated with a blue jay sitting on a branch against the standard glossy black ground, impressed mark, 10" ....**$400-$600**

Sabrinian, pillow, sea horses along the sides, stamped mark, 7" x 7-1/2" ....**$200-$300**

Selma, bulbous, decorated with daisies and butterflies, impressed mark, 4-1/2" x 4-1/2"...**$300-$500**

Selma, carved with squirrels, owls, and bluebirds in a tree, impressed mark, 7" x 4-1/4...**$600-$900**

Selma, bulbous, daisies and butterflies, impressed mark, 7-1/4" x 4-1/2" ....**$450-$650**

Selma, ovoid, with hooded owls under a crescent moon, unmarked, 8-1/2" x 4-1/4"...**$750-$1,250**

Sicard, bottle shape, rare, decorated with pine branches, marked on body, 13-3/4" x 6-1/4".......................................**$1,250-$1,750**

Sicard, bud, triangular opening, with stars and moons, marked on body, 4-1/2" x 2-3/4"...**$450-$650**

Sicard, bud, decorated with flowers, marked on body, 5-1/4" x 2-1/2" ....**$400-$600**

Sicard, cabinet, four-sided, daisies, marked on body, 4-1/2" x 2-1/2" ....**$400-$600**

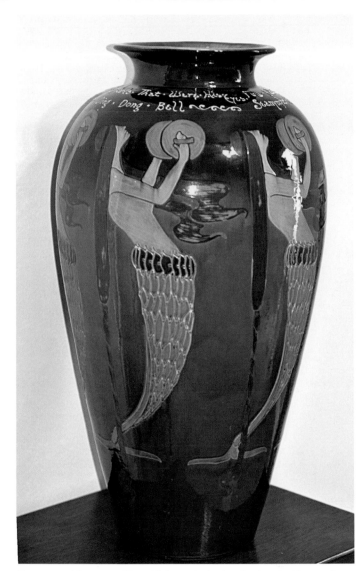

Monumental floor vase, Rhead Faience, incised and painted with nymphs holding cymbals and a motto in squeezebag, incised Rhead Faience mark, 26", value undetermined due to its rarity.

Sicard, corseted, decorated with foliage, overfired around base, 6-1/4"
....**$300-$400**
Sicard, floor, fine and large, with lilies, marked on body, 26-1/4" x 15"
....**$4,000-$6,000**
Sicard, gourd shaped, with flowers and dots, marked on body, 3-3/4" x 3"
....**$500-$700**
Sicard, gourd shaped with dandelion leaves, marked on body, 5"**$400-$600**
Sicard, gourd shaped, with peacock feathers, perfectly fired, marked on
    body, 5-1/2" x 5"...**$750-$1,000**
Sicard, gourd-shaped and painted with cornflowers in gold, perfectly fired,
    marked on body and impressed mark on bottom, 7-1/4"....**$750-$1,000**
Sicard, pillow, decorated with spider mums, marked on body, 10-1/2" x 6"
....**$1,250-$1,750**

Vase, Sicard, gourd shaped with dandelion leaves, marked on body, 5", **$400-$600**.

Sicard, twisted, decorated with clovers, very nicely fired, marked on body,
    5" x 3"..**$750-$1,000**
Sicard, twisted, decorated with flowing lines, unmarked, 5" x 2-1/4"
....**$500-$750**
Sicard, twisted, decorated with clovers, nicely fired, 5-1/2".....**$800-$1,200**
Sicard, tapered, has falling leaves, marked on body, 5" x 3-1/2"...**$600-$900**
Silvertone, covered in a matt green glaze, 7" ....**$400-$500**
Silvertone, bulbous, pink chrysanthemums, ink stamp mark, 9" h, 5-1/2" h
....**$395**
Silvertone, cylindrical, pink and white flowers, ink stamp mark, 8" h, 3-1/2" d
....**$300**
Silvertone, flaring, calla lilies dec, ink stamp mark, 11-3/4" h, 5" d.......**$375**
Silvertone, gourd-shaped, twisted handles, decorated with yellow flowers,
    stamped mark, 6-1/2" x 6"....................................**$300-$400**
Silvertone, two angular handles, pink and white flowers, Silverton and
    Weller paper labels, 10" h, 5-1/2" d **$300**
Souevo, squat, with geometric design in black and white, unmarked,
    4-1/2" x 7"..**$100-$200**
Stellar, squat, ivory with blue stars, rare raised marking, 5-3/8"...**$650-$850**
Stellar, bulbous, blue, painted by Hester Pillsbury, incised mark and artist's
    initials, 6" x 6-1/2"...**$700-$900**
Stellar, ivory with blue stars, marked in script, 6-1/4".............**$600-$800**
Tutone, three-sided, unmarked, 9" x 5-1/2" ....**$250-$350**
Tutone, rare, green leaf design around the rim, 12-3/4" ....**$500-$800**
Velva, brown, lidded, marked in script, 11-1/4" x 6" ....**$350-$450**
Warwick, footed, cylindrical body, unmarked, 10" x 4-1/2" ....**$150-$250**
Warwick, pillow, stamped mark, 10" x 7".........................**$100-$200**
Weller Matt Ware, two-handled with swirled design, incised Matt Ware mark,
    8-3/4" x 7"...**$400-$600**
White and Decorated, pear-shaped, painted with cherry blossoms,
    impressed mark, 7" x 4-1/4"..................................**$200-$300**
White and Decorated Hudson, painted with a band of roses around the rim,
    impressed mark, 7-1/2" x 4-1/4" ....**$100-$150**
White and Decorated Hudson, tear-shaped, painted with berries and leaves
    on a cream ground, impressed mark, 8-3/4" x 4" ....**$250-$350**
White and Decorated Hudson, faceted, painted with bands and clusters of
    light and deep pink flowers, impressed mark, 11-1/4".........**$300-$400**
White and Decorated Hudson, tear shaped, painted with blueberries, three
    of the leaves sketched but not painted in, impressed mark, 11-1/2"
....**$450-$650**
Woodcraft, corseted, has branches of fruit, unmarked, 12" x 6"...**$350-$550**
Woodcraft, double bud, owl perched on the top, impressed mark,
    14" x 7-1/2" ....**$500-$750**

Woodcraft, fine, tall tree-shaped with a squirrel climbing down the side, and an owl in the tree, unmarked, 18" x 7-1/4" ....$1,000-$1,500

Woodcraft, tall, branch handles and an owl in a tree, impressed mark, 13-1/2" x 5-1/4" ....$750-$1,250

Woodcraft, tree-shaped, impressed mark, 10-1/2" x 4-1/4" ....$75-$150

Xenia, ovoid, white circular flowers, 5-1/4" ....$1,250-$1,500

Vessel

Atlas, light yellow, bulbous, marked Weller C-3, 4" x 6" ....$200-$300

Baldin, brown with a wide, squat body, 7" x 9" ....$500-$700

Claywood, open, with fish, unmarked, 2" x 3" ....$150-$250

Ethel Creamware, flaring with ring handles, overflowing baskets of flowers, and maidens, unmarked, 11" ....$200-$300

Etna, squat, has two crossed handles, decorated with pink blossoms, impressed mark, 4-3/4" x 8-3/4" ....$250-$350

Knifewood, carved with swans and cattails, unmarked, 3-1/4" x 5"
....$300-$500

L'Art Nouveau, squat, nude woman wrapped around the rim, unmarked, 4"..$500-$1,000

Lonhuda, squat, painted with a brown tulip, stamped mark, 4-3/4"
....$200-$300

Louwelsa, squat, painted with clover blossoms, possibly by Madge Hurst, impressed mark and illegible artist's mark, 3" x 5-1/2" ....$100-$200

Vase, Lonhuda, tall and bottle-shaped, painted by Helen M. Harper with yellow flowers, green leaves, and buds, impressed mark and artist's initials, 13" x 6", **$450-$650**.

Vase, unusual, deep brown glaze drips on a white ground, numbers in crayon to bottom, 8-1/2", value undetermined.

Vase, yellow, bulbous, with incised marks on the body, and white leaves around the rim, kiln stamp, 7", **$600-$800**.

Vase, blue high-glaze, bulbous, by Dorothy England, 8-1/2", **$850-$1,250**.

Vase, unusual, ovoid, dripping glaze in bright yellow and blue over a pale blue ground, impressed mark, 10-1/2", value undetermined.

Experimental vase by Dorothy England with ruffled, scalloped, and braided edges on the tall painted body, marked, value undetermined.

Louwelsa, squat, painted by A. S, with branches of wild roses, impressed mark, 3" x 5-1/2" . . . . **$200-$300**

Louwelsa, three-footed, painted with nasturtium, impressed Louwelsa mark, 6" . . . . **$150-$250**

Matt Green, squat, incised with Native American designs, impressed mark, 5" x 6" . . . . **$750-$950**

Patra, handled, incised mark, 4-3/4" x 6" . . . . **$100-$200**

Sicard, squat, decorated with gold berries and leaves, marked on body, 4-3/4" x 7-3/4" . . . . **$600-$800**

Silvertone, squat, embossed with pink roses, strong color, stamped mark, 6-1/2" x 6-1/4" . . . . **$450-$650**

Turada, oil lamp-shaped, impressed mark, 6" x 9-1/2" . . . . **$350-$550**

Turkis, flaring, marked in script, Turkis paper label, 8-3/4" x 6" . . . . **$100-$200**

Warwick, unusual basket shape, stamped mark, 7" x 7" . . . . **$150-$250**

Wall hanging, Woodcraft, rare, with branch-shaped pockets, decorated with large pink flowers and applied blue birds nesting in branches, impressed mark, 15" x 13" . . . . **$1,250-$1,750**

Wall pocket

Blue Drapery, 9" . . . . **$200-$300**

Bonito, unmarked, 10-1/2" x 6" . . . . **$450-$650**

Fairfield, impressed mark, 9" x 5" . . . . **$100-$200**

Florala, conical, unmarked, 9-1/2" x 5" . . . . **$250-$350**

Glendale, imp mark, restoration, 12" h **$250**

Glendale, cornucopia shaped, stamped mark, 12" x 6" . . . . **$400-$600**

Greora, marked in script, 10-1/2" . . . . **$250-$350**

Klyro, basket-shaped, unmarked, 5-1/2" . . . . **$75-$150**

Klyro, tapered, unmarked, 6-3/4" . . . . **$75-$150**

Orris, embossed with a bird under a dark brown and green mottled glaze, unmarked, 8" x 4-1/2" . . . . **$150-$250**

Orris, with flowers and trellis pattern, unmarked, 8" x 4-1/2" . . . . . . **$100-$200**

Orris, trellis-form, large flowers in brown and green glaze, 8" . . . . . **$100-$150**

Parian, in pale blues and ivory on a grayish ground, unmarked, 8" x 4-1/2" . . . . **$200-$300**

Parian, in pale blues and ivory on a pale gray ground, unmarked, 10-1/2" x 6" . . . . **$300-$500**

Roma, with swags of red roses, impressed mark, 7-1/4" . . . . **$100-$150**

Roma, decorated with large basket of pink flowers, 10-1/4" . . . . . . **$150-$250**

Wall pocket, Orris, embossed with a bird under a dark brown and green mottled glaze, unmarked, 8" x 4-1/2", **$150-$250**.

Souevo, on Parian blank with black bands on a brown ground, unmarked . . . . **$100-$200**

Souevo, conical, unmarked, 12-1/4" . . . . **$200-$300**

Tivoli, conical, impressed mark, 9-3/4" x 5" . . . . **$75-$150**

Warwick, stamped mark, foil Weller label, and Weller Warwick Ware paper label, 11" . . . . **$150-$250**

Woodcraft, red flowers on a branch, unmarked, 9" . . . . **$300-$400**

Woodcraft, decorated with an applied squirrel, a very nice example of this form, impressed mark, 9" x 4-1/2" . . . . **$350-$500**

Woodcraft, large with owl in a tree, a very crisp example, unmarked, 10-1/2" x 6" . . . . **$300-$400**

Woodrose, unmarked, 6-3/4" x 3" . . . . **$75-$150**

Water jug, Louwelsa, spherical, painted by Frank Ferrell with an ear of corn, impressed Louwelsa mark, 6-1/2" x 6-1/4" . . . . **$250-$350**

Resources

There are many resources available to buyers today that make collecting and dealing pottery a much easier and more enjoyable hobby or career.

The Internet has introduced a new aspect to buying, giving access to thousands of pieces at one time through venues such as eBay, live online auctions, and dealer's Web sites.

It has also provided buyers with the means to obtain information on pottery, and connect with other buyers and sellers through online forums or discussion boards.

One excellent reference, online and offline, is the AAPA, or American Art Pottery Association, offering identification assistance, chat boards, and links to individual dealers, auction houses, shows, and conferences. The Web site is: http://www.amartpot.org/

For those seeking something more personal than an Internet sales room, one place remains a favorite among buyers and sellers alike: the Pottery Lovers Convention in Zanesville, Ohio, held every July. This show is ideal for those looking to browse the inventory of hundreds of sellers at one time, attend seminars on Ohio Pottery, and bid at several live auctions, all in or near the town it first began. It is the biggest and best show of its kind. More information can be found at http://www.potterylovers.org/

Grove Park Inn in Asheville, North Carolina holds an Arts & Crafts Conference every winter, with nearly a week of shows, lectures, and numerous other events. The L.A. Pottery show offers a great variety of pottery twice a year, as does the "Atlantique" City Show, in Atlantic City, NJ.

In the 1970s and '80s, very few books could be found on the subject of Weller or any Ohio pottery for that matter. Today you can find over a dozen books and price guides, along with hundreds of auction catalogs devoted solely to the history and wares of the Ohio River valley.

Bibliography

Bassett, Mark. *Introducing Roseville Pottery*. Atglen, PA: Schiffer Publishing, 1999.

David Rago Auctions. Assorted Auction Catalogues. Lambertville, NJ: 1986-2006.

Evans, Paul. *Art Pottery of the United States*, 2nd edition. New York: Lewis and Feingold, 1987.

Huxford, Sharon and Bob. *The Collector's Encyclopedia of Weller Potter*. Paducah, KY: Collector Books, Rev. 1989.

Purviance, Louise and Evan, and Norris F. Schneider. *Weller Art Pottery In Color*, 2nd edition. Des Moines, IA: Wallace-Homestead Book Company, 1971.

Purviance, Louise and Evan, and Norris F. Schneider. *Zanesville Art Pottery In Color*. Leon, IA: Mid-America Book Company, 1968.

Perrault, Suzanne and David Rago. *Miller's: American Art Pottery: How to Compare & Value* (Millers Treasure or Not). London, UK: 2001.

Snyder, Jeffrey B. *Weller Pottery*. Atglen, PA: Schiffer Publishing, 2005.

Wunsch, Al and Linda Carrigan. *Weller Pottery: The Rare, The Unusual, The Seldom Seen*. Sarasota, FL: Marlin Media Publishing, 2003.

Subscribe Today

GET ONE FULL YEAR AT A GREAT LOW RATE! 1 YEAR (52 HUGE ISSUES) $38.00

That's right. Try *Antique Trader* today and discover the most authoritative voice in the antiques world. Each issue's filled to the brim with valuable information for your pursuit of antiques.

You'll find…

- Current prices and values
- Dolls, toys, furniture, clocks, glass and all special interests
- Exclusive antique market trends
- Auctions tips, techniques and strategies
- Expert appraisals
- And much, much more!

Don't pay $155.48 at the newsstand.

Subscribe Today & Save 76%!

DON'T WAIT–
Log on to www.antiquetrader.com and subscribe today.

Call 877-300-0247; outside the U.S. & Canada, call 386-246-3434. Offer code: J7AHAD
Or write us at: P.O. Box 420235, Palm Coast, FL 32142-0235

In Canada: add $71 (includes GST/HST). Outside the U.S. and Canada: add $121 and remit payment in U.S. funds with order. Please allow 4-6 weeks for first-issue delivery. Annual newsstand rate $155.48.

Enhance Your Collecting Know-How

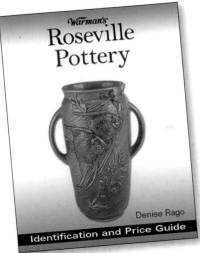

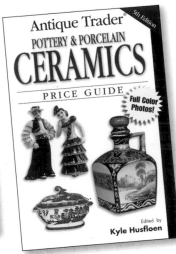

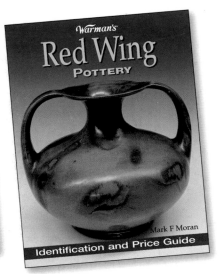

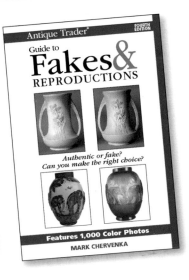

Warman's® Roseville Pottery

Identification and Price Guide

2nd Edition

by Denise Rago

Inside this comprehensive Roseville reference, written by America's leading expert, you'll discover all the details needed to make the most of your collecting. With 1,800 color photos, company history, an up-to-date market report and a compendium outlining proper procedure for caring for pottery, it's clear this guide is unmatched in its depth of detail.

Softcover • 8-1/4 x 10-7/8 • 288 pages • 1,800 color photos
Item# Z0781 • $24.99

Antique Trader® Pottery and Porcelain Ceramics Price Guide

5th Edition

by Kyle Husfloen

Explore both U.S. and European made pieces from the 18th century through the mid-20th century, current values, detailed descriptions and more than 3,600 color photos in this all-inclusive reference.

Softcover • 6 x 9 • 768 pages • 3,600 color photos
Item# Z0327 • $24.99

McCoy Pottery

A Warman's Companion

by Mark F. Moran

Perfect size for taking to antique shows. This new book offers solid collecting data including company history, values, 1,000 color photos, and tips for spotting fake McCoy pieces.

Softcover • 5 x 8 • 272 pages • 1,100 color photos
Item# CCMC • $17.99

Warman's® Red Wing Pottery

Identification and Price Guide

by Mark F. Moran

Brilliant full-color photos showcasing 1,200 pieces of Red Wing stoneware, art pottery and dinnerware are accompanied by current pricing, historical facts, detailed descriptions.

Softcover • 8-1/4 x 10-7/8 • 256 pages • 1,200 color photos
Item# RDWG • $24.99

Warman's® Hull Pottery

Identification and Value Guide

by David Doyle

Avoid losing money on fakes and forgeries by referring to the detailed descriptions, 800+ color photos and Hull pottery history featured in this new guide.

Softcover • 8-1/4 x 10-7/8 • 256 pages • 800+ color photos
Item# Z0334 • $24.99

Antique Trader® Guide to Fakes & Reproductions

4th Edition

by Mark Chervenka

This full-color, one-of-a-kind guide for spotting fakes and forgeries rescues you from making costly collecting mistakes in today's reproduction riddled antiques and collectibles market. With 1,000 detailed photos comparing originals to reproductions you will find page after page of sound advice for identifying forgeries.

Softcover • 6 x 9 • 368 pages • 1,000 color photos
Item# Z0723 • $24.99

krause publications
An imprint of F+W Publications, Inc.
700 East State Street, Iola, WI 54990-0001

To order call **800-258-0929** Offer ACB7

Pick up these and other Krause Publications antique and collectible reference books at booksellers and hobby shops nationwide, or by calling the publisher directly at 800-258-0929 and mentioning offer ACB7. Visit Krause Publications online at www.krausebooks.com to view other antiques and collectible references.